Unconditional Love

Unconditional Love

A Guide to Navigating
the Joys and Challenges of
Being a Grandparent Today

Jane Isay

HARPER

An Imprint of HarperCollins*Publishers*

FIRST EDITION

Designed by Bonni Leon-Berman

Library of Congress Cataloging-in-Publication Data has been applied for.

ISBN 978-0-06-242716-8

18 19 20 21 22   LSC   10 9 8 7 6 5 4 3 2 1

To the Nine of Us

A POEM FOR EMILY

Small fact and fingers and farthest one from me,
a hand's width and two generations away,
in this still present I am fifty-three.
You are not yet a full day.

When I am sixty-three, when you are ten,
and you are neither closer nor as far,
your arms will fill with what you know by then,
the arithmetic and love we do and are.

When I by blood and luck am eighty-six
and you are someplace else and thirty-three
believing in sex and god and politics
with children who look not at all like me,

sometime I know you will have read them this
so they will know I love them and say so
and love their mother. Child, whatever is
is always or never was. Long ago,

a day I watched awhile beside your bed, I wrote this down, a
thing that might be kept
awhile, to tell you what I would have said
when you were who knows what and I was dead
which is I stood and loved you while you slept.

—MILLER WILLIAMS

CONTENTS

....

Unconditional Love

INTRODUCTION: STARDUST

Look into the night sky. See those stars twinkling? Every time a child is born, a new star shines in the firmament. Big bang theory tells us that all matter came into being at the same instant. All matter began as stardust, and that's what we are made of. It's a romantic idea, I know, but easier to imagine if the new star is a grandchild. The specialness, the charm, the brilliance, and the beauty—this is magic for grandparents. When each of my grandchildren was a baby, I informed the parents how advanced the baby was, in all ways. See? He's already focusing? Look at her. Did you ever know a two-week-old who smiled? You know the rest. They call it "Grandma vision." I was right, of course. It just took months or years for the parents to see what I saw in my arms from the very start.

Grandparents over time get accustomed to their special duties: slow down; listen carefully and respond thoughtfully; sing the old songs and tell the family stories. Play infinite card games and reread favorite books until they are committed to (failing) memory. Grandparents have a serious responsibility to hug and to snuggle, to play what the child wants to play, and to help the spirit flourish.

For many grandparents, this is the opportunity to become the parent they didn't have the time or the energy to be with their own children. Burdened with the inevitable demands of raising children, needing to be in two places at the same time, running the household and accommodating hectic schedules, we found it almost impossible to devote enough thoughtful time and attention to our children, no matter how hard we tried. We ran out of patience and we ran out of steam. If we remember with regret those moments—and many of us do—then here's our second chance. Babies arrive with a clean slate, which we can fill with the patience and acceptance we may not have been able to give our children.

Eye Contact

WHEN MY FIRST grandchild was a tiny baby, I spent one morning a week watching him so his mother could get a break. She left me little packets of pumped breast milk, in case he got hungry. I was so glad when he wanted to eat. I loved to hold this small person in my arms and look into his eyes. It changed my whole body. I relaxed, I felt warm and easy. Those big black eyes were blank at first. I didn't mind. My eyes were not blank. They were filled with joy at the miracle in my arms. Soon his eyes began to wander, looking at a light, or at a leaf. When his eyes would move toward my face, I could see a minuscule bit of baby comprehension. I sang him a song while he glanced at the leaves. I learned the song from watching *Mr. Rogers' Neighborhood* when this baby's father was a child: "Tree, tree, tree." Maybe you remember it. A few notes and a few words. The baby would catch the sound of my voice and turn to me. Then his eyes would wander back to the leaves on the tree behind the couch.

It was such a peaceful time. These moments of eye contact changed me. They made me experience relaxed love for the baby and trust in the return of his love. Unconditional. All I had to do was hold him, feed him, love him. How could it be otherwise? The baby had no knowledge of me, my flaws, my personality, my relationships—all the things that make me worry or feel bad. He gave me nothing to criticize or worry about: an infant has a big future but not much of a past.

Stardust. Unconditional love is the magic bridge that spans the generations: we love them unconditionally, and they love us back without reservations. It's a two-way experience. It grows the children and gentles the grandparents.

Stardust is the feeling, but family is the reality. We are flesh and bone, and we have history and memory. We have conflicts and resolution. We have joy, and we have sorrow. In this magical mix of the generations, we consider what it is to be a grandparent, and what it takes to keep our conflicts to a minimum and our joy at the maximum.

Today more grandparents and grandchildren are enjoying this joyful bond than ever. The statistics are startling. Baby boomers are the beneficiaries of demographics, economics, and medical progress. The richest generation in American history, we are financially more secure than those who came before—or after—us. Beneficiaries of the longest life expectancy in American history, we can expect to be part of our grandchildren's lives for a very long time. Finally, we boomers have the opportunity to participate in the rebirth of the connected family. I say rebirth because family closeness took a big hit in the decades after World War II.

American Diaspora

IN THE SECOND half of the twentieth century, our country underwent what I think of as the American Diaspora. Before World War II, we had been a largely agricultural society, with vast swaths of farmland and overcrowded cities bursting with tenements. Families lived together out of need. They stayed together to work the farm or lived in crowded slums to stay safe and off the street. Then things changed.

In the years after World War II, America experienced extraordinary economic growth. Veterans married, and their children became the baby boom generation. Developers built millions of houses in the areas outside the cities and created our suburbs. In unprecedented numbers, people poured out of the tenements and into the suburbs, leaving their elder relatives.

Veterans who qualified (it took years for African-Americans to receive this benefit) went to college and graduate school on the GI Bill of Rights. At the same time, businesses expanded all over the country, and they needed employees. Manufacturing, given a big boost because of the war effort, went into high gear. Good jobs were available to people who were willing to relocate. Who would turn down a promotion to be close to Mom? Please. America soon became the most mobile society in the world.

Then the psychologists and psychoanalysts, subscribing to the beliefs of the day, undermined the notion of the family. In this period, families of origin were believed to be breeding grounds of mental illness. Mothers were blamed for everything from schizophrenia, to homosexuality, to autism (check the old textbooks—this is true). Loosening the family bonds was a step toward improved mental health.

By the time baby boomers went to college, they expected to live apart from their parents following graduation. Sons and daughters of immigrants ran toward assimilation. In this era, friends became more valued than family. People dreaded going home for the holidays. Given a choice, they would choose any community but the family. "We get to choose our friends," boomers would say. "We're stuck with our families."

But the economic trials of the twenty-first century have diminished this Diaspora. Great numbers of grown kids live at home after college, for longer than anybody anticipated. And now surprising numbers of grandparents move near their children and grandkids, instead of going south or west for the good weather. Grandparents have become an important resource for many families.

Many grandparents help out with the grandkids. In great numbers they offer time or money, and in some cases both. Their help is needed. Two working parents are the rule now, not the exception. Grandparents today are in better physical shape than ever, thanks to improved preventive medicine and healthy living. Because of increased life expectancy, we may be alive to attend college graduations and even offer toasts at the weddings of the grandchildren. Having four (or six, or eight—if there's a divorce or two) living grandparents is no longer rare for young adults. Great-grandchildren may even brighten our lives. We live at an extraordinary time, when opportunities to burnish the experience of being a family are immense. And so are the challenges. Aware of both, we enter a new time of life.

Three Stages of Grandparents

WE GRANDPARENTS COME in three age groups. And there are differences in the way we relate to the youngest generation. Young grandparents, still at work with busy lives, and probably with spouses, don't have much time to linger with the grandchildren. Perhaps they will visit with their family, on weekends and on trips. It is a wonderful thing to have grandchildren when you're not old enough to qualify for Social Security. You may not be able to spend days on end with the babies, but you can be pretty sure that you'll be able to attend one of their graduations—and even a wedding. As you'll read in the pages that follow, the pleasure of time with grown grandchildren is also magic—in a different way.

The middle group of grandparents may have it the best: they have the time and the energy to crawl around on the rug and play catch in the backyard. Many also have the mental and financial resources to travel the world, save the world, and still have a chance to come home to tell bedtime stories. We age as the grandchildren grow up, and the natural rhythms of our lives seem to be in sync. I'm in this group. My first grandchild was born the month before I turned sixty-five. I had just left my last paid job a few months before. Three other grandchildren followed in lively steps. I don't have to pick them up anymore, and they are patient with me now, as I was patient with them in the past.

Elder grandparents, the people whom we think of as matriarchs and patriarchs, are slower to get out of a chair, and if they are lucky enough to have many grandchildren by the time they are elders, they may not remember everybody's name and birthday, but they may be in line for a new generation—great-grandchildren.

The age of the grandchildren also informs how we relate to them. When they are babies, access has everything to do with our grown children, their parents. Our relationship with those families, warm or cool, relaxed or tense, sets the stage. It comes as a shock to many grandparents that the parents have total control over our access to the babies. As we adjust to this shift in power, we can see the bones of our past rise again in the new family, for good or ill. As the grandchildren grow, they have more of a say in whom they want to spend time with, and for how long. They still need the consent of the parents, but they are beginning to assert control. And finally, when they're grown, grandchildren can come to us independently.

Grandparents know that the most concentrated time with the grandchildren is when the parents are out of the room. Kids relate to us in a clearer and more intimate way when we are alone with them. It's also a nodding truth that these close relationships are built one on one. Time alone with a grandchild is golden. The flow of love is unmediated because there are no distractions. Attention is complete. Sometimes it's exhausting. And taxing. I think of the two marble lions that sit in front of the main branch of the New York Public Library. They are named Patience and Fortitude. That's us.

About This Book

THE BOOK BEGINS with the announcement of an impending birth and follows the life cycle of today's many three-generation families. I have interviewed members of all three generations in an attempt to learn where the problems are and how people solve them. My focus, after years of being a grandparent and of talking with all my friends and listening to many kind people who sat for interviews, is that while we are no longer in charge, grandparents can, with our perspective and experience, find a way to keep the love flowing.

I'm in favor of:

Conversation, even though it can sometimes feel overwhelming.

The long run, where people decide to heal their breaches in order to be together.

Acceptance, even though it may be difficult to achieve.

I think that:

Most of us try to do our best, and need to be forgiven
when we fail.

Secrets and surprises may tilt the boat but don't
necessarily sink it.

Grandparents and their grown children are happier
when they give each other the benefit of the doubt.

The advent of grandchildren offers families the opportunity for healing and redemption—if we seize the moment.

While working on this book I read about a book that had been published in Germany called *The Hidden Life of Trees*. The author, Peter Wohlleben, is a forester who worked for decades in a small forest, which he studied while he managed it. He was surprised to learn over his years of tending to trees that the closer trees are to each other, the healthier they are. Their roots, we learn from Wohlleben, communicate underground, furnishing neighboring trees with the needed chemicals and substances that contribute to their survival. He tells us that the underground roots of nearby trees nurture the stumps of dead trees for centuries. The lesson of the trees is this:

Near or far, our families nurture life. Obvious or hidden, our connections with each other can heal and sustain. Whether we like it or not, we are part of our family. Our lives will not last as long as the trees we love, but our families will endure. We can help each other, across the generations, with our attention and affection. The stories that travel down through the years nurture our descendants long after we're gone. We contribute to this continuity by the acceptance we offer and the time we share. It's our immortality.

I hope that what follows will help you to deepen your roots so that you and your family can experience all the pleasures of life across the generations.

PART I

The Family Grows

1

Grandparent Prep

Grandmother (that's me—I'm in need of a hug):
"Come here, darling, I have a secret." Mazie
   comes for a hug and hears, "I love you."
"That's no secret, Grandma."

We were celebrating our younger son's birthday at a New York steak house. My former husband and I always turned up together on these occasions. A family is a family, we agreed. When the wine was served, I offered a toast to the birthday boy. His wife looked on with a smile. And then Josh raised his glass. Here's to you, Grandma and Grandpa. What?

Why was he referring to my parents this night? They had died long ago. Then a look of recognition ricocheted around the table. He was talking to us. They were going to have a baby, and we were going to be grandparents. My former husband said he was too young to be a grandfather (he was nearly seventy years old). I got weepy and thought about baby presents. A grandmother! I would have pictures to carry around, stories to tell, a baby to hug and to love. I always believed that a grandchild would be my immortality, a person I had loved who would tell my stories, sing my songs, and remember me long after I was gone.

When Josh called me Grandma that day, my mind slipped back to the moment of his birth. And then I experienced a set of Pinterest images: Josh in the stroller, his dark eyes obscured by the swath of blond bangs; at the dining room table beating me at gin rummy before his feet could touch the floor; collecting shells and rocks, and talking, talking, talking—even in the bathtub when the rubber ducky was his sole audience. We watched the TV news together. I remember how we leaned on the pillows of the big bed. I thought about all the experiences we had shared.

Then I tried to picture the child my son and his wife would have. In my imagination, I snuggled the tiny head on my shoulder, and I smelled that amazing newborn mix of spit-up and baby powder. I saw myself walking the baby back and forth to calm it, and I thought of all the songs I had been sung, the songs I sang to my son.

That night at home, my fears set in. How would my second husband deal with the fact that he was going to have to share me with yet another person? Would he love the baby even though they weren't related by blood? Would the tension between him and my sons keep me away from the baby? The reality of a new person in the mix was scary.

Would the baby be healthy? Ten fingers and ten toes? What kind of parents would my son and his wife be? Worries filled my heart, and then came the regrets. I had let my son down when he was a teenager, and I'd never apologized. Would he hold that against me when he became a parent?

How much time would I want to spend with the grandchild? I'd just retired from my last full-time job weeks before, and I was thinking of writing a book. Would I have the time to be with the baby? Enough time? Would my kids want me around? We had a good relationship, but divorce and remarriage had busted wide open the image of an inherently close family. Josh's wife came from a big family, and her parents were still married, and she was close to her siblings and her parents. She was already an aunt, so her parents were much more sophisticated about all matters grandparent. Would I be the odd grandmother out? Would I earn a passing grade?

I felt as if I were sitting in an empty movie theater. All my concerns were projected onto a great big screen, and I was in the dark. But I had six months to chew over all these issues. And so does every new prospective grandparent. Worries and excitement create a strong emotional mix.

I realized that everyone who is soon to become a grandparent has some work to do. First we need to assess our family situation. Then comes the work of memory, followed by the work of information. Finally, we may strive to accomplish the work of acceptance.

Assess the Situation

THE ARRIVAL OF a baby changes the family dynamic, but the old relationships that have been laid down years or decades before play a decisive role in the way in which we behave as grandparents. Consider these questions:

Do you and your partner welcome the new baby with similar enthusiasm?

Do you agree about the commitments you plan to make on behalf of the new family?

If you both still have jobs, how do you plan to make room and time for the grandchild?

If you're retired and enjoy the pleasures of a life of ease, are you ready for the disruption?

If you have other grandchildren, do you worry that you won't have time or energy for the next one? (I know people with a dozen grandkids, and they have trouble remembering each child's name. That's not lack of love, but it's a different climate from the tiny family of Mom and Dad, two children, a dog, and a cat.)

What about the in-laws? They will play a bigger part in your life, now that a baby is on the way. If everybody gets along, that's great. But cultural, racial, religious, and gender differences may come into play. Since the other family will be important in your grandchild's life, you are likely to spend more time together than you did before. You're not a bad person for feeling tense, but you'd be a wise person to let go as much as you can.

Life in the twenty-first century is different from the way we grew up. There's a much wider range of love choices for young adults, and sometimes those decisions create a challenge for the grandparents. We aren't making the love choices. Our choice is whether or not to welcome the new in-law and the new family into our lives. We have decades ahead of us, and if we want to be included, we might start by being inclusive. Open arms will keep us welcome in the nursery.

Hal's Irish parents are fervent Catholics. When his brother brought home a Protestant girl, his parents were severely unhappy, and they showed it. They refused to attend the wedding and wouldn't accept their new daughter-in-law. So Hal's brother and his wife moved across the country. His parents saw precious little of the grandchildren until the divorce. Now Hal's niece and nephews journey to spend time with their grandparents, but his parents lost years of pleasure and connection with their only grandchildren.

If you were unhappy with your grown child's choice of mate and showed it, the months leading up to the baby's birth might be a good time to try to deal with the old wounds. Here's a first—but not the last—chance to make peace. First, you might try to become more accepting of the one you rejected. You might consider an apology, for the early unfriendliness. A gesture of acceptance might not hurt. A significant effort to take responsibility for any early negativity may soften the lingering resentment. The movement away from the old tensions can be slow. But there's nothing wrong with gradual—so long as progress is made toward genuine ease.

The distance between grown children and their parents is not uncommon in our culture. Kids have been expected to leave for college and not come to live at home again, unless there's a problem. Young couples are building their relationships, their careers, and their circles of friends. They don't have much time for their parents—except for holidays and other important occasions.

I've heard from many parents of their frustration over this: They don't pick up the telephone. They don't respond to e-mails, and some won't even respond to a text. What to think? These kids are busy, just plain busy. It's also important to understand that men and women in their twenties and thirties are still finding themselves as adults, and they need to separate from the family, just the way two-year-olds and adolescents do.

Hard emotional work is daunting—and exhausting. We all go through this, in one way or another. Nobody is perfect in their family relationships. Nobody. We all have work to do, and some of the work lasts a lifetime. But the task can become less taxing as we notice just a tiny bit of progress, a sense that the atmosphere isn't quite so tense this time. Perhaps it's a moment where everybody is charmed by the baby's smile, or delighted at the way the fat thighs kick when the baby notices something new. I can't tell you when and where, but I believe that the very presence

of this new creature can soften hearts, if we are serious
about our intention to create peace where there was none
before. Now that we have assessed the emotional climate
in our family, it's time to look backward for a moment and
think about how we got here.

The Work of Memory

YOU CAN DO this while you take a walk, or ride your bike,
or drive to work. Perhaps while you putter around or listen
to your playlist. Take a trip back in time and return to
your early weeks of being a parent.

Remember the day your first baby was born. Were you
scared? Did your parents help, did they intrude, or were
they absent? Go back to those frantic days after the baby
came home. Remember the exhaustion when the baby was
awake and the worry when the baby slept too long. See
if you can re-create in your imagination those crazy six
weeks or so, until the alien you brought home turned into
a person.

Elizabeth, grandmother of three, had lost her mother
by the time she had her first child. Her husband's mother,
the beloved Nonna, came to help the new parents out. "I
remember the day Nonna went home. She was with me for
a week, and my husband had gone back to work by then,
and I remember the baby was sleeping, and I remember
walking out to the driveway with Nonna and thinking,
'You can't leave now.' I remember the car driving down the
street and the hole in the pit of my stomach."

As I listened to Elizabeth's story, I experienced a physical reaction. I felt the anxiety all over again. And I was envious of Elizabeth's relationship with Nonna.

My parents and my in-laws just weren't those people. They sat by the telephone, perhaps, but not in the hospital waiting room. Many of my peers had the same experience. We weren't crazy about having our mothers participate in these intimate moments. In the 1960s and 1970s, we didn't trust anybody over thirty.

Baby boom grandparents are the living exemplars of the Second Chance. It's a grand opportunity to use our past, and our children's past, to create a sound and loving future.

Take another step, back to your childhood. Perhaps you still have the photo albums your parents kept of you and your siblings when you were young. What do you remember about your parents and your siblings? Can you bring to consciousness your sense of the household in which you grew up? This is useful because so many of the strategies we employed to raise our children—the future parents—came as a response to how we felt we were treated as children. Those memories will clarify some of our guiding principles, and why we chose them.

I grew up in a family of Freudians, who were quick to interpret anything I had to say—with their meaning, not mine. It was infuriating. And when I tried to hold my own, and argued with the reigning interpretation, I was told that the very vigor with which I defended my position proved that I really didn't believe what I was saying.

So when we were about to have our first child, I informed

the future father, a psychoanalyst in the making, that there would be no place for Freud at our dinner table. None. The kids' feelings were to be respected. If they didn't like somebody, they were told they had to be polite, but their emotions were not to be negated. As I followed this rule, I corrected my parents in retrospect and hoped to make it easier for my children. I hope we created an atmosphere for our boys to grow into who they were bound to be.

Respect for the feelings of their children is not always so easy for parents. But for grandparents, this is a walk in the park. We are so interested in what they have to say and in what they feel. It's our job to recognize who they are. And that is what helps kids and young people become who they must be.

By giving our children what we lacked, we got to rebalance the scales. So take some time to think about what you loved as a child—and repeated as a parent. Then remember what wasn't so great. Even allow yourself to grieve over some of your childhood sadness. You'd be amazed at the power of memory. When you remember something from yesterday, you may be taking away its power to control you today. This will be useful when you become a grandparent.

Now reconnect in some detail with the parent you were, decades ago. Did you just adore the babies, or did you get happier when the little ones could walk and talk? What kind of temper did you have? Were you explosive or calm? What aspects of your parenting are you proud of, and what do you regret? This time travel will help prepare you for the moments when you observe your children as parents. If you pay careful attention, you will see how they repeat the experiences they remember with joy and avoid situations from their childhood that they didn't like or resented.

Mining for Gold

SEE IF YOU can find the time before the baby is born to reminisce with your kids about their childhoods. The information you get will be spectacularly useful when they become parents. And maybe, just maybe there will be some truth telling in the conversation (perhaps over dinner and some good wine). Our memories are selective, and frankly there are too many events in the growing-up years for family members to remember everything that went on. The stories grown kids remember—and tell—are likely to differ immensely from ours. That's not a problem. It's a path to greater understanding. Keep in mind that everything is subjective, and that nobody in the conversation has the one, real truth. Breaking down walls is the point. Being right is a side issue.

One of the tasks that grown children need to accomplish (and often don't, by the way) is to reimagine their parents as regular people, not the authorities who always judge, not the people with the megaphones who shout out directions and point out dangers.

So a conversation in which family members recall the roses and the thorns of the past is a step toward a new mutual understanding. And it offers an additional boon for

your child's partner by opening a giant window onto the
family that person has joined. The more you can share,
the better. It might even be possible, in the course of these
conversations, to clear up some of the inevitable misunderstandings about things that happened in the past.

This is gold. Remember together funny and fantastic moments, disappointments and successes, ups and
downs and everything in between. Maybe there will be
talk about the aunts and uncles, the grandparents, and
the cousins. What a joy it is to create a newly shared past
in these conversations. If the kids disagree about what
happened when Jamie broke the window, and when Mom
threw the tantrum in the car on the way to California,
that's fine, too. Resentments about forgotten things we
did to our children may well emerge. We can take it all in.
And by learning something about how our own children
remember their childhoods, we will have a better notion
of what we can expect from them as parents.

You might even solicit some stories from the new family
member: What did you love as a child? What did you hate?
What's the mythology in your family? What will you sing
to the baby? Imagine the power of these questions asked
and answered. Somebody once said, "Listening is an act
of love."

Finally, as you complete the survey of your family tree,
think about your own grandparents. What kind of relationship did you have with them? So many grandparents
have told me that their own grandparents were a major

influence in their lives. Grandparents furnish our DNA and also create the culture we inherit. If you loved them, know that your grandchildren will love you. If they didn't speak English and you still found a way to communicate, appreciate how wide a vocabulary of love you will have with your grandkids. If they were standoffish, see if you can understand why. Every generation plays a part in the formation of our role as grandparents. Some of this we remember, and some of it is unconscious. But all of it will come together to form our new grandparent selves.

The Work of Information

THE NEXT STEP is to learn how today's parents are raising children. Reminiscing about the days when our children were small is good fun, but our memories are attached to the way things were. Check out the experiences of your friends who are already grandparents. Talk to them. What surprised them most about the new child-raising mores? What were the hardest parts for them? Such conversations will both reassure you and alert you.

Times have changed, and it's useful to be fully acquainted with the mores of the day. Here are some old-school beliefs that will stun anyone now going through pregnancy.

I drank and smoked when I was pregnant (laughter).

We could test for Down syndrome, but not much more (heads tilt in disbelief).

Amniocentesis was the only test available and not used much.

We were given vitamins, calcium, and iron pills, and nothing else.

Some of us were told not to swim, lest germs creep up inside of us.

Rubella (German measles) was the great scourge—and we had no way of knowing its effect on the fetus.

The blogs and the Web sites you visit will acquaint you with today's rules of pregnancy and all the tests pregnant women now take. A friend of mine who is pregnant told me that her panel of genetic tests covered two hundred genetic diseases. Some of these diseases weren't even discovered when her mother was pregnant. It's wise not to shrug at all the worries our daughters carry until the test results come back. Chalk this up to progress, and stay positive.

While you're at it, you might just check up on today's baby and child care advice. A lot of it comes from their friends and advice offered on social media. The future parents will trust Facebook and blogs, Twitter, and Instagram—and maybe read a book or two. The more we know about what they believe, the more prepared we will be to understand their rules and worries. An informed grandparent is also kind of hip.

Think of this kind of work as preparation for a long voyage to an exotic spot. Read the books, check out the Web sites, and talk to people who have been there.

More informed about the way things are done today, we may not feel the need to instruct the new parents about the truth as we lived it. It's important, because if there's one thing adult children don't love, it's advice from their parents. Here's why. The people we raised hear our suggestions as criticism, even though we don't mean to be critical (do we?). New parents, frantic and sleepless, are supersensitive. On the other hand, they can hear praise very well. And they are eager to be told that this baby is the most amazing, gorgeous, wonderful, adorable being on the planet. So let the comments be full of wonder about the baby and full of praise for the ways in which they are coping with the unknown. When we emphasize the positive, we have a major impact. Praise is not only noted and appreciated, but it also reinforces good feelings between generations.

The Good-Enough Granny, or The Work of Acceptance

GROWING FAMILIES ARE under tremendous stress for time and money. Many grandparents come to their aid and delight in the new intimacy that often occurs after the arrival of grandchildren. But like all adults, we make our choices. We decide how much time to spend with the grandchildren. How important are they in our lives? Do they come first? Do our significant others share our enthusiasm for the expenditure of time and money? Or do we need or want to continue our lives as before, with occasional visits to the grandkids, some phone calls, gifts, and no family earthquakes? These questions are asked and answered many times over the decades. Don't forget that we have choices.

This book is written to help both adult generations—grandparents and parents of the grandkids—deal with the conflicts, problems, and politics of family life. But we live in a world where women especially are expected to be perfect. Let it go, friends. If your best friend babysits her grandchildren four days a week and you want to see the grandchildren four times a year, it's all good.

I grew up in the 1950s and never was thin enough or tall enough. When I look at the snapshots from that time, I see a lovely young woman with big brown eyes, looking for acceptance. I worked when my children were small, and I never felt that I was in the right place: when I was at home, I should have been at work, and when I was at the office, I should have been home. We lived in a university community, and it was the time of "competitive casseroles," a dinner-party culture that kept faculty wives in the kitchen. The fact that I worked was a mark of Cain. It was made clear to me that I couldn't be a good mother. Like every woman of my generation—and yours—I know how it feels to flunk the perfection test. Fortunately, a British psychologist, a great expert on infant-mother attachment, came up with a most comforting and excellent concept:

"the good-enough mother." Oh, how I love Dr. Winnicott. He let me know that perfection is an illusion. In his honor I offer his concept to the elder generation: the Good-Enough Grandparent.

So let yourself off the hook, even after reading about all these exercises and mental gymnastics. It's going to be fine, and the years will be your best teacher. Families are the bedrock of the human species. All we need to do is love, and breathe, and it will be all right.

Now, Breathe

SIT QUIETLY AND take yourself back in time to the months when your child was first born. Breathe in and out. Bring back to mind the agony of not knowing how to calm the fussy newborn. Remember your panic when the feeding didn't go right. Breathe. Now bring to your mind what it felt like not to shower, to nurse endlessly, to be up all night with a fussy baby and then wake up again when the newborn had slept for just a few hours. Pant. Bring back to your mind the smell of newborn spit-up and the mountain of dirty Onesies that seemed to grow when you weren't looking. Deep sigh in and out.

Then you will tread softly in the home of your children.

Then you will empathize with the new parents' panic at their loss of control.

Then your sympathy for the new parents will abound.

Then you will control your desire to take over and do it your way.

Then you will be compassionate and loving—even when provoked.

Then your heart will burst with the joy of watching your child become a parent.

2

When Everything Changes

Holding that new baby for the first time is a singular moment. It's a miracle. With that miracle comes a host of new experiences and cosmic changes in the family. The baby and its parents are not the only people who face challenges and opportunities to grow. Grandparents stand at a threshold.

It's not just a new baby. The new parents are changing in plain sight. The couple may have raised a puppy, or a kitten—I know a couple who were raising chickens—and thought they were training for parenthood. What the new parents are discovering in those first hours and days is that they are not playing house anymore. They have to take responsibility for a new human life. They have to grow up, like it or not. Recently a writer in the *Atlantic* posed a question to readers: Can you tell when you become an adult? A surprisingly large group of people in their thirties responded that it was the moment when they became parents.

I remember the moment of my gut realization that this new creature was my responsibility. It happened in the hospital when they left the baby in my room for the day. I was exhausted and scared and I wondered how I would have the strength and wisdom to care for the helpless little alien next to me. Somehow I did, and so did all the grandparents reading this book: that little baby, so helpless and scary, is our grandchild's mother or father.

The ordinary give-and-take of life is amplified in the first few months of the baby's existence. Over time the new parents learn that a pimple is not scarlet fever and that a loose poop is not a sign of fatal diarrhea. The grandparents probably knew that, but it takes some tact to express such superior knowledge without making the parents feel stupid. Yes, it's walking on eggshells, but it's also a way to acknowledge that our children take their new responsibilities seriously. It's a time to accept them as adults. That's so hard. Our natural instinct, when our children are under stress, is to help them by taking charge and making everything right. When they are confused and exhausted, they may feel to us as if they were children. But they aren't. They are adults. These young people, suddenly beyond their depth, will learn to overcome their fears and inadequacies. They will deal with the challenges. We did, after all. Those early months are great training for those of us who need to give up trying to make everything right for our grown children. If we can master this self-control, we will grow along with them.

The new parents are thrilled and frightened, sleepless and anxious. They know how little they know, and they realize that they are in charge, even as they are overwhelmed by the responsibility. And because they are so intimidated by the presence of the small creature they now have responsibility for, new parents are often rigid about following rules: their rules, not our rules.

These rules may come from Twitter, from Instagram, and from blogs—all of which they consider to be authoritative. New parents often become literal and territorial. If the blog says to nurse for seven minutes on each side, the timer rings, and the baby is switched. When the time is up, no more nursing. Pediatricians suggest that new mothers buy notebooks in which to record when the baby was fed, for how long, and when the baby pooped.

Grandparents don't remember doing this, if we ever did, and we have a pretty good idea that the infant will eat and grow, and poop, cry, and sleep, and eventually become a proper baby, whose behavior is easier to understand and predict. Grandmothers who are helping out with the new baby walk a narrow path. On one side is the knowledge that experience brings, and on the other is the danger of downplaying the new parents' concerns. "Give me the baby, I'll calm her down" can offer the new mother relief, or it can be misinterpreted as criticism of her ability to parent.

Bringing Up Grandma and Grandpa

AS THE NEW parents assume the responsibilities of caring for a child and feel the growing pains of responsibility, they may need the help of their parents in many ways. But they do not enjoy the experience of feeling helpless and incompetent. They need to grow their confidence and to relax. Eventually they do.

The elder generation may also take the opportunity to grow. Becoming a grandparent is the crowning event for many people, so why should it present a challenge? Because the rules are about to change, and promoting harmony in the family under new circumstances takes patience and modesty. It requires that the elder generation adopt a long view.

We grandparents need to recognize and accept that the new responsibilities of parenthood bring new power—to set the rules. Many of the rules may seem silly to us, but if we disrespect them we also disrespect the people who set them. It takes self-control to abide by the wishes of our grown children, when we have so much more experience and the broad perspective of time. But as we respect their wishes and follow their rules, we send a signal that we understand the shift of power that is taking place. In this situation, as in many, respect makes life easier and keeps the welcome mat out.

When Elizabeth was walking on the beach with her pregnant daughter, the young woman asked her if she would be willing to watch the baby once she was ready to go back to work. Elizabeth was thrilled. She tells me that the eighteen months during which she took care of that baby while her daughter was at work were among the happiest of her life. Divorced early, Elizabeth had to work full-time to support her daughters and never experienced the rich pleasure of taking care of a baby, day in and day out. She enjoyed every minute.

Now the granddaughters are both in elementary school, and Elizabeth picks them up from school several afternoons a week. "How do you deal with rules?" I asked, knowing that the two adult generations sometimes clash over feeding and discipline. "It's easy," she said. "I follow my daughter's rules. The girls take off their shoes in my house, even though they don't need to, because that's what they do at home. Why should they have to remember two sets of rules?" Simple, isn't it? Elizabeth has put harmony first.

When we babysit the grandchildren in their own home, sometimes the kids take over and make it hard to abide by the parents' rules. Becca came home from the theater with her husband one night to discover that her two children, three and five, were still running around the house—at 11:00. They had just shared a good-size chocolate bar under the supervision of their grandmother! It would be hours until they calmed down and went to sleep. Even if they went to bed late, Becca knew that they would be up at dawn. When she asked her mother what happened, she heard this: "Well, they didn't want to go to bed, so your father and I decided to let them watch TV, and then they asked for a treat. What could I do, they begged for the chocolate."

Three strikes and you're out? The kids stayed up too late, they watched more TV than allowed, and they got caffeine-laden chocolate just before bed. Becca knows that everybody will survive this, but she wishes her parents would be a little more responsible with the kids. She wonders if the price of two fussy children the next day is worth the night out. Maybe next time she'll get a babysitter who follows her instructions. Becca gets to decide next time: Will she ask her parents and deal with the ensuing chaos or will she pay a stranger and expect calm?

The In-law Conundrum

THERE'S ANOTHER TWIST in the new-generation story: mothers-in-law need to tread ever so carefully. It's a plain fact that the matrilineal line, mother and daughter, is more powerful than the mother-and-son connection. Research over the decades has shown this, and most mothers of sons will attest to its truth. The mom of the baby is usually the Decider. And if she's not comfortable with the way in which her husband's mother behaves around the house, there will be trouble. Who needs trouble at this time of joy—and anxiety? A mother behaves differently in her daughter's home because she knows her. She raised her. They have fought and reconciled for decades. A mother knows where the land mines are buried.

It's different for mothers of sons. The same small issue that would raise an eyebrow between a grandmother and her daughter can cause trouble between a new mother and her mother-in-law. And the new father is not likely to come to his mother's defense. His focus is on his wife, and properly so. It's an old story. The house of our grown children is not our territory. We don't necessarily have a key to that kingdom when the baby arrives. The kinder we are, and the more support we offer, the easier it is on our children, and the warmer our welcome will be. This is especially true with daughters-in-law. So many women have told me how they have to court the daughter-in-law and work all the time to create an easy back-and-forth. I was chatting with a friend who is in her eighties and has ten college-age grandchildren. When I mentioned the need to establish such a relationship, she cocked her head to the side and said, "I'm still courting her."

The issue of respect and regard is so important to the daughter-in-law because she's the newcomer into her husband's family. She has not shared a lifetime of conflict and resolution, the way she has with her own mother (remember her tone when she said, "Mother, please!"). She may feel that she still is on trial with her husband's family— especially now. She remembers if she was welcomed into his family or if things didn't go so well. (Note to grand-parents: if some of your children haven't yet connected with a spouse, remember to be gracious to everyone they bring home. As they say, "Hey, you never know.")

She is likely to be more comfortable with her own mother. That makes sense, and it's not unusual. Recognizing that this is more than common may relieve us of taking her preference for her own mother personally.

Since she comes from a different family, she may have been raised with different traditions of child rearing. This is a time for learning, not criticism.

She will be sensitive. And she will notice both our words and our actions. Even while she is changing the newborn's diaper, she won't miss an odd expression of ours, or body language that signals disapproval. Praise, love, understanding, and gestures of respect are the keys to intimacy in this dynamic.

Why should I do this? you might ask. She's his wife, but I'm his mother. That's true, but she and your son have the power to welcome you into their lives or to distance themselves and their children from you. So we need to be aware of how the smallest slight can grow in memory.

Angela is still nursing her baby, who is now six months old. She and her husband are happy to go over to her in-laws, who are celebrating their wedding anniversary. It will give Angela a chance to show off her daughter. Angela is so proud, and she can dress the baby in a lovely outfit her in-laws gave them. The baby is beautiful, and serene.

They are welcomed with much joy and festivity. Cake is being served, and it's time for Angela to nurse the baby, so she repairs to the study with her infant. "She needs to try the icing!" her mother-in-law says. "Thank you, no. She isn't eating any solids yet." Undeterred, Angela's mother-in-law offers to hold the baby while Angela buttons herself up, and what does Angela's mother-in-law do? She slips a finger full of icing into the baby's mouth. Angela will not forget. It's symbolic of the way these people behave. She's not going to trust them.

What's the matter? you might ask. It's only a bit of icing. The new grandmother was excited at her party and perhaps just a little tipsy from champagne. Give her a break. You have a point. But think of this: at a time when every rule is a matter of life and death, disregarding such a rule is a slap in the face. This sense of being disrespected lasts longer and stays at a higher level of intensity than we might anticipate. If the in-laws don't respect something so obvious as not feeding icing to a newborn, how can the parents trust them to be responsible about anything else? If years later these grandparents invite the grandchild out to a meal or an event, can the parents trust that their children will be urged to order healthful foods?

Some daughters-in-law are anxious in ways that surprise the elder generation. Gail invites all her children and the grandchildren to visit her and her husband at their summer house on a lake on Michigan's Upper Peninsula. It's about as beautiful a spot as you can find. As you might expect, it's all about the water: swimming, boating, playing around, splashing, and getting accustomed to a rural scene. The cousins have to be hauled out of the lake when they get cold (remember "your lips are blue"?), and they love the chance to drive the boat—under adult supervision, of course. Gail was looking forward to the visit from her son, his wife, and the two-year-old. Then she got an e-mail from her daughter-in-law.

> I'm really concerned about getting pressured to have Georgie in the water, on boats, on docks, or on the rocks. If I feel that I'm getting pressured or asked why or criticized, I'm just going to leave. He cannot swim and does not need to be in a lake, on a dock, or in a boat. I don't care if other people have infants on boats, but I am not that reckless.

"Well," Gail tells me, "at least I'm prepared." She would agree to follow her daughter-in-law's edicts to the letter. Gail isn't going to let this woman's concerns keep her from her grandson. There will be an older Georgie on another summer visit, when they can ride the boat and frolic in the lake.

Margo, visiting her son soon after the first baby was born, thought she could be of help if she washed the pile of dirty dishes and scrubbed the filthy pots in their kitchen sink. The new mother, seeing this, was enraged. "Stay out of the kitchen," she warned. What? Margo was helping. But Margo had crossed a line she didn't even know existed; she had moved into her daughter-in-law's territory. What her daughter-in-law meant was, "stay out of *my* kitchen!" Her son's wife mistook the cleanup as a judgment about the mess she had left. Margo learned over time to take her daughter-in-law's sensitivities into consideration.

Most of the tension between the generations comes from behavior that isn't life endangering. But signs of disrespect from the in-laws are taken with utmost seriousness. Outside of stepping in when we notice a threat of bodily danger to the baby, no dispute is worth weakening the family bond.

Robert Frost said it: "Good fences make good neighbors." Mindful of the boundaries between us and our grown children, we make the effort to take the differences between us less personally. If we leave our old habits behind, we can ease the transition for our growing, grown children and our maturing, mature selves.

We remind ourselves daily that this is all about access. Access to the baby. It helps to be aware of three major hot spots.

Food Fights

WE LIVE IN an era of intense scrutiny about what children eat. Sugar is considered by many parents to be a poison. People who are old enough to be grandparents may remember when other foods were off the menu—and then on again. Eggs were killers, now they're good. Butter, that supertool of taste, was replaced by margarine—until margarine was found to be full of bad chemicals. So butter is back. Red meat has just turned up again as something that may be OK, in moderation.

So for us a dab of icing, an extra cookie, or a breakfast of Froot Loops may not loom as clear and present dangers. And furthermore, most children love sweets. So why not give them what they want? Here's why:

Jamie will never forget the kindness of her in-laws. They minded her children while she was recovering from surgery. The twins were infants and her daughter was two years old. Jamie reclined on the couch every day and watched with gratitude how those grandparents cared for the children. But when her in-laws fed her daughter bowls of super-sweet cereal, it made her blood boil. Jamie's own parents were hippies, and for them sugar was more dangerous that climbing high trees or riding bareback. She agrees. Because she was not in a position to complain to these generous people, who were after all caring for everybody, she gritted her teeth. Today, at their house, they still stock the kitchen with Frosted Flakes for Jamie's teenagers. Jamie still seethes. She felt a degree of hostility in their refusal to listen to her, and while there's still gratitude for how they helped her when the children were tiny, she watches these people with a certain suspicion.

Then there's the matter of fresh versus cooked. I was raised in a city, and the vegetables we ate were either canned or frozen. Fresh vegetables came into my life after I got married. I would never eat canned peas or serve frozen asparagus again. Fresh is good, to me. But cultures differ.

Janice's son married a Russian woman, whom she doesn't much care for, but that's not the issue, she tells me. They are raising the children in a bilingual household, so the children speak Russian and English. The mother and maternal grandma talk to each other in Russian, which Janice doesn't understand, so she isn't in on the conversation between them. Her son and the grandchildren speak English with Janice, so she's not totally out of the loop. But what annoys her most is the food. Her daughter-in-law cooks the Russian way. Janice tells me that everything is brown, overcooked, tasteless, and not good for the grandchildren. Do they seem badly nourished? Not at all, but where are the raw and steamed veggies? Janice's disapproval of her daughter-in-law's cuisine is obvious. Meals when she visits are tense.

Food fights between the generations can be unremitting sources of irritation to both generations. If we take the long view that the grandchildren will survive with or without the cuisine we cherish, then there may be a little less tension at the kitchen table.

The Wrong Stuff

AMY IS A tenured professor and a busy woman. She and her husband struggle to keep up with the needs of the kids, the household, and their careers. Her mother, a loving woman, comes to the house laden with gifts for the grandkids. The basement is bursting with toys, games. Little bits of plastic from the dark ages turn up from under the rug and behind the couch. Amy can't stand it. Nothing she says will stop the flow of stuff.

She has begged her mom to quit it, and she tries to keep the latest delivery from reaching her children, but when the kids see the bags full of presents, they ignore their parents and go right for the stuff.

Amy has nightmares that if she leaves the tiny pieces of plastic alone in the basement, they will mate and propagate when the moon comes out. She admits that she can't manage the flow of crud. She and her husband can barely get the laundry done and the children fed and put to bed each day. Her mother doesn't have to clean up after the children. If she did, she might understand the look in Amy's eyes when she arrives laden with presents.

Callie was raised to believe that possessions are less important than people. How come her parents, who imbued her with these values, are doing the opposite with her children?

Callie's parents come to see the grandchildren once a week. She wishes they were more engaged with her kids, talking with them, playing with them. Instead they bring gifts and then turn on the TV. Cheap, crappy bags of plastic arrive weekly. Callie tells me that she and her husband worry about too many possessions. Living in this ultra consumer culture, they are trying to raise their kids with the values they grew up with—the very values her parents taught. So why do they seem deaf to her requests for No More Stuff? She shakes her head.

It's hard on children when relatives come with gifts that infuriate their parents. They can't understand why their mother and father are angry about Grandma's generosity, and they want the presents. They're kids. Kids want more. They want too much. That's why they have parents. And understandably, the parents don't want to have the grandparents put them in a bad light for living by the values they are trying to instill in their children.

Poor Grandma Nina fell victim to the gift debacle. Her son and his wife feel strongly about controlling what their children get. People who are raised abroad, like her daughter-in-law, may recoil at the amount of stuff American children have. The event happened when Nina came back from a trip to Europe, laden with gifts. The magnificent platter of cheeses she schlepped from Italy was rejected before the cellophane could be removed. Nina had ignored her daughter-in-law's requests on so many levels. To Nina's daughter-in-law, presents of any kind are anathema. Cheese is not a healthy food. She went ballistic when she saw what Nina had brought. She took the platter away from the children, despite their tears. This was a bad time for everybody. The daughter-in-law now allows Nina to visit for just two days twice a year. Nina tried to talk with her son about this, but he doesn't respond. Whether or not the marriage is strong (Nina has suspicions), Nina's son sides with his wife. This is a fact of family life.

To Be(d) or Not to Be(d) and Other Deep Matters of Discipline

THE GRANDCHILDREN ARE sleeping over. Bedtime at home is 8:30. It's now 10:30 and they are still up. Grandma and Grandpa are by now tired, so putting everybody in front of the TV seems a satisfactory solution. There are plenty of good reasons to indulge the children—especially on weekends. After all, we're not living in a gulag. Nobody will suffer if the children are a little tired in the morning, and maybe they will sleep past dawn. Enjoy. But expect that the parents, when they learn about this, may not be thrilled.

The grandchildren are visiting the farm. All the kids of previous generations learned to drive the tractor before their feet could reach the pedals. Grandpa throws them all in the back of the pickup truck to drive around the property. The back of the pickup truck doesn't have seats, much less seat belts. What's a parent to do? These conundrums of everyday family life are hard to resolve. But a canny grandpa can tell the parents' reaction in a flash. If it's OK, that's wonderful, but if they look anguished, then maybe a change of plan is in order.

This sounds like an etiquette lesson for grandparents, and it is. The reason to be mannerly with the middle generation is clear: access is theirs to allow or withhold. And sometimes, maybe they are right. But right or wrong, they are the parents. Being careful not to go over the line with the grandchildren makes good sense. And if a difficult divorce has caused tension among any family members, it makes sense to exercise particular care. If family members aren't close to start with, there is danger of a rift.

Keeping close to the grandchildren after divorce takes even more sensitivity. Do you see those amber lights flashing? Annoyance over the divorce, disapproval of the child's manners, criticism about the ex's parenting skills—these judgments get communicated through body language and attitude. Here's a cautionary tale. Small things get magnified when there's tension. Ryan's grandparents lost access to him over a trip to the lobster shack.

Ryan was visiting his father's parents. The divorce happened years ago. These grandparents never cared for Ryan's mother. They think she and the other grandparents spoil him rotten. Still, they invite Ryan for an occasional weekend at the beach. One Saturday, Ryan didn't feel like going with his cousins to the lobster shack on the dock. He was involved in a video game and thought nothing of staying put. The grandparents were furious, and so that night at dinner, as punishment, Ryan got a hot dog on his plate while everybody else ate lobster. Ryan's mother made sure that this would be Ryan's last weekend with his paternal grandparents.

Why We Spoil

IT CAME AS a surprise to me that so many people resent their parents' actions toward the grandchildren. Their vehemence was a shock, and so was their seeming inability to change their behavior. From parents I heard "It makes me crazy." I heard "Why don't they listen?" And sometimes I found people who limited the amount of time they allowed their children to be with the grandparents. From grandparents I heard "I'm only welcome in their house for a day or two, and then I have to go home." I heard, "She doesn't like me." Most of the disputes seem to be over things like food and discipline and gifts, but the subtext is really about respect and boundaries. Why do so many grandparents ignore what their grown children ask? Is it a response to relinquishing power? Is it a relic of the time when that grown child was an annoying teenager and we thought, "Wait till you have children. You'll see." Are we asserting our power through sugary cereal, unappreciated gifts, and too much screen time?

In our defense, three dynamics make it hard not to indulge the grandkids against their parents' wishes: culture, our life history, and that certain smile.

The culture is full of messages that instruct grandparents to spoil the grandkids. You can see it on Facebook and grandparent Web sites, blogs, and social media. Doting grandparents are an enormous market for toys and other gifts. Industries are built on this. Have you ever been to Build-A-Bear? It's a brilliant invention, a clever and purposeful money drain for grandparents. All the merchandise fits all the bears, and who can resist a child's desire for a pair of sunglasses for the bear, even if it costs four

dollars. Not to mention American Girl. A pair of doll sunglasses will set you back ten dollars.

This cultural message isn't only for the wealthy. Grandparents who don't have a lot of money bring bags of stuff
from Walgreens, or collect old toys from yard sales.

People living carefully on their savings will invade
their small 401Ks for new skis. Loving grandparents indulge grandchildren. It's who we are. And that's what
the blogs tell us, and what our friends and neighbors report. It's what we are supposed to do. It's what we want
to do.

But there's a difference between helping and indulg-
ing. The baby boom generation of grandparents by and
large is more affluent than their children and grandchildren. Many grandparents help out financially, but that is
a different species of giving, which you'll read about later
in the book. It's the giving despite the parents' express
wishes that pushes buttons.

Second, our life history plays a major part in our inability
to hear what the grown children are saying.

Here's Eugene, who loves his two grandkids more than
life itself. He was raised by his grandparents during the
Depression, when his father would leave town to find work
wherever he could. The boy and his grandpa were insep-
arable. The whole family lived in western Tennessee, on a
large tract of land. Eugene was homeschooled by his educated grandmother, who was a teatotaler, and his grand-

father taught him farm skills when he was very little. He could handle a horse at five and drive a tractor at six. Eugene's grandpa liked his whiskey, but his wife couldn't know. So grandfather and grandson hid the bottles around the farm. Sometimes Grandpa would forget the hiding place, but not Eugene. This was their secret. Oh, how they loved being coconspirators.

Fast-forward. Eugene, now the grandfather, phones his two grandchildren every evening, counts the days until his visits, and suffers when they are apart. The parents feel strongly about sugar, and the little boy doesn't get cookies. Maybe he can have one from time to time, but his parents are the Deciders. So what does Eugene do? He arrives with a secret stash of cookies, and when the parents are not around, Eugene hides the cookies along with his grandson. It's a game they play together, and they have a lot of fun looking for the treats and eating them. Is this so terrible? Ask his daughter-in-law.

Here's another one. Geneva picks up her grandson one day a week after school. She's lucky, and so is the little boy. They romp. But the first thing that happens when he arrives at her house is the Popsicle. If he wants one, he goes downstairs to the freezer and takes his pick of flavors. It's nothing, right? Except that Geneva's daughter and son-in-law have always struggled with their weight. They're trying not to make this an issue with their stocky little boy, and so they encourage him to be involved in all kinds of sports activities. Sugar treats are not part of the program, and they are working at keeping this from being a source of unhappiness at home. He's got the energy of a dozen kids, but he's somewhat overweight. Geneva's daughter depends on her parents for afterschool hours, and she's grateful, but she can't understand why her parents refuse to abide by her wishes. They are smart, educated, loving people, and they adore the grandchildren.

It turns out that Geneva's memories of her own grandmother may be at work. She tells me about a grandma she adored. Geneva, the oldest of four, always volunteered to help Grandma with the dishes. That's where she heard the family stories and imbibed a deep sense of family history. Side by side they stood, one washing and the other rinsing. Geneva would say, when the task was nearing completion, "Grandma, could we do the dishes a little slower?" Geneva had a lot of responsibility for her younger siblings, and it exhausted her. But she was a good oldest sister, and a good girl. One thing about Grandma's house puzzled her. "Grandma," she asked, "how come your cookie jar always has my favorite cookies in it?" You know the answer, and so do I. Years later, there was no way Geneva could deprive her grandson of a sweet.

The insecurity of age is the third reason why grandparents don't listen to their grown children when it comes to gifts. We treasure an excited reception when we arrive. The "Grandma!" The grin. The run that ends in a hug that almost knocks us over. There's nothing like it, and for people who are attaining the elder years it has a special significance. Older people live in a world where we are becoming invisible. I walk down the city streets, striding like a young person, and the teenagers don't see me. Sometimes I think I'm in danger of being knocked down. It's not just the iPhones. Groups of kids walk together and almost bump into me. A nurse at my physician's office, hearing my age, said, "Bless your heart." In stores, and at cash registers, the clerks call me "Sweetie." I haven't figured out a polite response to that one. Once I mumbled "I'm not sweet at all," and the clerk at Whole Foods gave me a weird look.

"Grandma!" means so much to me. And when I picture arriving at the house, and seeing the children, I imagine the extra delight if I come with a gift. I used to bring presents to my grandkids when I visited on Sundays, usually appropriate items such as books or art projects. I figured they would lighten my daughter-in-law's burden on a Sunday afternoon. Then one day I arrived empty-handed, and Mazie asked, "Do you have a present for me, Grandma?" "No," I said, "I don't." I felt terrible. And she looked sad. "Grandma's come for dinner," her mother said. "That's gift enough." My daughter-in-law, ever the diplomat, was sending me the message: enough with the presents; I don't want the kids to have that attitude. I heard her, and I realized she was right. My granddaughter still asks, but she's so glad to see me, even empty-handed, that it doesn't seem to matter anymore.

The Intangibles

THERE'S A GREAT world out there of intangibles we give our grandchildren. These intangibles don't cost anything and have no calories. Most of these intangibles are unintentional. They come as a delicious consequence of our love and attention. You'll see what I mean in the next chapter.

PART II

The Intangibles

3

Nurturing the Moral Imagination

Unless a fellowship of spiritual experience is
re-established, a parent [or grandparent] will
remain an outsider to a child's soul. We appreciate
what we share, we do not appreciate *what we
receive.* . . . Friendship, affection comes about
by two people sharing a significant moment, by
having an experience in common.
—*Abraham Joshua Heschel*

My friend Mary and I have been discussing the concept of
the moral imagination for decades. We have talked about
our grandchildren (she has five, and I have four) for fif-
teen years now, and after stories of their charm and brilliance, we settle down to thinking together about their
manner of being in the world. We call that nurturing
the moral imagination because it's a way to capture the
underlying ethics they carry with them—their ability to
put themselves in the shoes of others, to understand their

own feelings, and to respond to the world with kindness and acceptance. That one sentence sums up the message of many religions. If only all people had the qualities of empathy, self-understanding, kindness, and acceptance, that would be my utopia, and perhaps your heaven. So let's allow ourselves to imagine that the attention and love we give our grandchildren can help them grow and eventually help to mend our troubled world.

The moral imagination isn't created by discipline, and it doesn't include following orders from the authorities. It doesn't identify with any particular faith. It is an internalized sense of self that connects with what is kind and fair, real and just.

Parents work hard to make their children into good family members, mannerly and responsible people. But parents are obliged to multitask most of the time. They prepare breakfast as they check for clean hands and neat clothing. They come home tired from the day's work and may need some quiet time when the children clamor for attention. They are responsible for discipline. They comfort their children when they are hurt or sad, and they constantly try to understand and nurture them. These conscious efforts are crucial to the success of their children and to the formation of a civil society. But parents can only do so much. That's where grandparents come in. By our ordinary attention, our unconditional love and acceptance, our endless patience and slower pace, we help to establish the four pillars of the moral imagination: empathy, perspective, knowledge, and agency.

Empathy

IT'S REMARKABLE HOW the everyday activities we do
with our grandchildren affect the kind of people they
will become. The ability to put yourself into someone
else's situation is nurtured by experiencing empathy from
others. Even before children develop self-awareness, an
adult's glance or gesture of understanding and acceptance
is received as a comfort. And who does that better than
a grandmother or a grandfather? In the hours we spend
with grandchildren, our job is to love them and have fun
with them. Sure, we may need to give a bath or help with
homework or encourage them to do their chores. But most
of the time we don't need to hustle them. Because they delight us, even their small infractions don't irritate grandparents the way they might get under the skin of busy
parents. Maybe we are more patient. Maybe, because we
have no overweening agenda, we can sometimes see the
grandchildren as they are, not as others wish them to be.

Teresa tells me that she knew she was different from
the time she was five years old. She had a crush on her
teacher, Miss Ogleby. She couldn't understand her feelings, and she certainly didn't like them, so she took this
as her burden. One day when her girlfriends were playing
dress-up with their mothers' clothing, Teresa, who only
dressed in slacks, just couldn't do it. She put on the hat

and the flowery skirt, but she couldn't get herself out the door. Tears, followed by self-hatred and then a promise to herself to keep her feelings secret from her strict Catholic parents: this was how she lived in the world.

The family shared a two-family house with Baba, Teresa's grandmother, who lived upstairs. Teresa went upstairs to Baba's room when she came home from school. Teresa was nine when she noticed a pair of brown patent-leather loafers in the window of a local store. They were boy's shoes, and they cost two dollars. Her mother wouldn't hear of buying them for a girl. Anyway they were too big. Every day as she walked home from school, Teresa would look at the brown shoes in the window and wish they were hers. She told Baba how much she loved them. She couldn't understand what was so terrible about wearing boy's shoes. Even though they were too big, she could stuff a sock in the toe of each shoe until she grew into them. Then one day they weren't in the window. Teresa shrugged and walked home.

When she got upstairs to Baba's, a brown paper bag lay on the kitchen table. "For you," said Baba. Teresa tore open the bag, and there were the patent leather loafers. "You can wear them up here," Baba said, "but don't ever tell your mama about them. If you do, I'll throw them away." Teresa understood.

The first thing she would do at Baba's was to put on her shoes. First they were too big, and then they were just right, and when they became too small, Baba sliced the sides at just the right spots so her toes could stick out.

That way Teresa got another few months' use out of them. Eventually they wore out, but Teresa's gratitude to Baba for love and recognition will never wear out.

Today Teresa is a minister and counselor who helps LGBTQ teens find self-acceptance. Baba, an immigrant from Germany who never learned to read, understood none of today's concepts—but she knew that little girl, and she loved her.

Some grandparents have the opportunity to bring some peace to a home that's chaotic. Beverly was one of ten children. You can imagine the complexity of the world she and her siblings inhabited. But there was one sanctuary: Granda's corner of the house. Granda lived with Beverly's family for the decade after his wife's death. Imagine this salty Boston Irishman living in a rangy stucco house in New Mexico with ten clamoring grandchildren. There was always a dime in Granda's pocket when they went to a ball game, and he spent summer days at the town pool watching the children. But the best gift of Granda was his ability to understand and accept. First thing all the children did when they got home was to visit Granda. The five minutes they spent with him were precious, the only opportunity each of them had to experience one-on-one focus and love.

Granda interceded with the parents when Beverly and her brothers and sisters got into trouble. He smoothed the waters, and even though he was a devout Catholic, when a grown grandchild chose another faith, Granda was there to help. He imbued in each of them a kind of understanding and generosity of spirit that has lasted Beverly and her siblings through their lives. And they have lived good lives. Many of them are dedicated to helping others, and they are still close.

Of course the parents had a major role in forming the character of their ten children, but Granda is the one who provided singular and sacred space where the children could feel accepted as individuals and therefore learn to accept others.

Empathy has tremendous moral power. When we begin to feel what another person is experiencing, it's harder to judge that person harshly. It's true for all generations, and we are always learning.

I walk my dog around the corner where I live in Manhattan, and for years I ignored the pleas of our local panhandler. In fact, I wanted him gone. He's big, and he looms over the corner. One large front tooth juts from his empty gums. He's got a wild curly beard and limps as he walks. He calls out YOU GOT ANY CHANGE in a loud, gruff voice. I don't carry money when I walk the dog, so even when my grandson Benji was with me, I would look the other way and pass him by.

This went on for years until something changed in me, and I decided that I couldn't ignore this guy anymore. The first time I gave him a dollar, he jumped up and said, "I finally qualify!" As I got to know him, we exchanged names and greetings. Benji and I sometimes talk about Wes, who lives in public housing just a couple of blocks from me. One day when we were discussing him, I realized that Benji didn't know what the projects were. And so began a discussion about public versus private housing. That day my grandson wasn't having any of my bleeding heart liberalism when I criticized the real estate moguls whom I blamed for the high cost of housing in New York. He told me that people had a right to make money. I didn't try to win the argument; Benji has a right to his opinion.

Over time, Benji got to know Wes a little bit and heard more about his story. He began to see life a little bit through Wes's eyes. The lessons of Wes continue. When Benji's little sister Ruby recently saw Wes with a cigarette, she worried that he uses some of the money I give him to buy cigarettes, which are bad for him. She thinks that I shouldn't give him money if he spends it on cigarettes. She says I should give to organizations that help poor people. From that came a lively discussion. Because of Wes we can consider charity, what happens to people who make mistakes in their lives, and the best way to help. So the corner panhandler is also present at the creation of my grandchildren's moral imagination.

Mary lives in Nebraska. She has at least a hundred trees on her land, and is profoundly tied to the natural world. A bird-watcher, she gave each of her grandchildren a guide to the birds of Nebraska before they could read. By the age of four, these kids could identify twenty or thirty different birds. They know when the shorebirds will come to eat the grain, and when to look for the fox who walks by their window. They have an encyclopedic knowledge of trees and flowers. I wish our grandchildren could trade places, so that hers could meet Wes and form their own thoughts about the tall, growly man who needs help from us. They would be intimidated by the noise and the crowds on Ninety-Sixth Street and Madison Avenue just as my grandkids would probably be a bit restless in the country, away from the hustle and bustle. But they might learn some names of the birds and the trees and the flowers. And they would wait for the fox with excitement. Both grandmothers agree that changing places would deepen the souls of both sets of grandchildren. City kids and country kids would have shared experiences. Empathy.

Perspective

ONE OF THE advantages of age, never mind the creaks and the meds, is perspective. By the time we're old enough to have grandchildren, most of us have lived at least half a century. Because of the rapid pace of modern life, we have experienced what our grandchildren consider "history." This is a delightful circumstance because of the response we sometimes get. "You lived without TV?" "No Internet?" It goes on. As we tell them stories of what the world was like when we were growing up, we help them set their lives in a broader context. Our lives, simple and complex, easy and hard, serve as models for them, partly because we are two generations removed.

Danny is thirty years old and still mourning the death of Oma, his grandmother. She was an amazing woman, he tells me. Born in Leipzig, she was five years old when the Nazis went on the rampage known as Kristallnacht. Oma's father somehow got the family out of Germany, and they landed in Ecuador, where they lived for decades. Eventually they got to the Bronx, where she met Opa. Sometime in her thirties, Oma discovered that she was going blind. Danny was the first grandchild, and the only one whom Oma was ever able to see. Persecution, exile, and even blindness—none of these stopped Oma. Danny tells me:

"The grandchildren viewed my *oma* in world historical terms. She had overcome unimaginable adversity. And I think the amazing thing about it was that she was OK. She was clever, she was charming, and she was everything you want in a person. She was also blind, but she didn't let it define her."

I asked him about her death, and he described the hospital room filled with family. They noshed and chatted and sadly but lovingly watched her heartbeat slow. Danny came away from that experience understanding the power of survival and family. He told me that, if he could imagine his deathbed, surrounded by a family he had helped to create, his life, too, would have meaning.

Oma had a Seeing Eye dog. After the death of her

husband, the dog was her closest companion and survival mechanism. In memory of her, Danny and his family donated money to train a Seeing Eye dog. They all attended the dog's graduation ceremony and watched as she met her new owner. The dog's name is Oma.

Without preaching, without scolding, Oma's stories set a living example for the grandchildren.

Grandmothers who grew up in the South during the years of Jim Crow tell their grandchildren of their experiences as children, setting a powerful context for the new generation. One grandma tells me that her ten-year-old grandson is astonished to learn that as a girl, his beloved and respected grandmother had to sit on the back porch of the Alabama home where her mother worked all day long, cleaning, cooking, and doing laundry. Why the back porch? That's the way the lady of the house would have it.

Grandmothers who were part of the Great Migration north tell their grandchildren how their fingers bled from the prickles when they picked cotton. The children are astonished to learn that Grandma was made to enter the local grocery store by the back entrance and to drink water from a separate fountain.

These common stories from the generation that lived through Jim Crow model endurance. There's no stopwatch governing progress in our world. But the grandmothers who tell the stories of their experiences in what the children may think of as "ancient history" provide a depth of understanding, not through books or screens, but by the loving and sometimes heartbreaking retelling of the stories of their lives. What makes these stories so vivid is that we lived them, and they are in our bones.

My friend Pam tells me that her grandfather, who owned a dry-cleaning shop in Chicago, had wanted to be a doctor. When he applied to medical schools, he was told that the Jewish quota had been filled. Pam was shocked. She had no idea. But she does know that her grandfather was a very smart and kind and wise man. That would have to do for his generation.

My grandchildren are surprised to learn that, as a VP of a major publishing house (and the only woman at the table), I was sometimes asked to serve the coffee at meetings. One morning I got into the office very early and a rug cleaner was at the door. "Can you tell me where the boss is?" he asked. "I'm the boss," I replied. I remember the shock on his face. These stories of personal experience with history are shocking—and revelatory.

If we can take them to visit the house we lived in, if we can share old snapshots from when we were kids, we connect them directly to our experience. I found a diary that my father kept in 1917, when he was a teenager. My grandkids hold it as if it were a fragile antique. In a way, it is. It is also a message in a bottle.

Our own lives give them courage. They see us going through our days, happy sometimes and sad at other times. The beauty of these lessons is that they're not taught in school but shared from one generation to the next. It's one of the ways in which we grandparents may enter their souls.

Knowledge

CHILDREN ARE SPONGES. And they are especially ready
to sop up what grandparents tell them. They observe every adult carefully, even as they go about their activities.
But there's a sacred space around grandparents and the
grandchildren where they share knowledge.

Knowledge is different from information. Information
is what you get raw from all kinds of sources, from books,
from various media, and in school. Knowledge is information processed through life experience.

I recently found myself trying to explain genetics to
my seven-year-old granddaughter. She noticed that the
crackers she especially loves for a snack after school are
low calorie and asked if that's why I have them. She's at
the prime age to begin worrying about her shape and
size, so first I reminded her that we love those crackers
because they are crunchy and make whatever you spread
on them taste better. Was I on a diet? she wanted to know.
I told her that while I'm a bit pudgy, my health and my size
seem to agree. She wondered what size she would be when
she grew up, and so I decided to tell her that our genes are
the best predictors of body shape. Hair? That was easy,
and so was eye color. Then it got a little complicated, and
I had to come up with some pretty inventive ways of de-
scribing systems that were scarcely understood by scien-
tists when I was her age. The conversation continued as
we walked the dog to our corner bookstore, where I asked
for the biography of Rosalind Franklin, who many be-

lieve discovered the double helix. That afternoon, I was informing her on many levels: I wanted to accentuate her confidence in her own body, I wanted to give her some understanding of what we can change and what we can't, and I wanted to introduce her to a great woman scientist. In other words, the information I gave her was processed by my love and concern specifically for her.

One Sunday morning my Brooklyn grandson and I chatted about how I was writing this book. I was in the leather chair and he was on the floor, creating a structure out of slats of wood. "You're not retired!" he said. "Right," I said, "but I did stop working in an office eleven years ago." "But you're still working. How come?" I told him I love my work and probably will stop sometime, but not right now. Then I told him about his great-grandfather who saw patients until 6:00 on the day he checked into the Coronary ICU a week before he died. I told him that his Pop Pop Dick had worked almost up to his last days, too. The conversation wafts through the playroom as his father passes by. "That's the kind of conversation you can only have with grandparents," he comments. Right. This offhand discussion will exist as a tiny shard of color in the great mosaic of his understanding. It didn't carry the weight of importance, but it enriched the context of his life.

Albert, now a retired physician, was pretty much raised by his grandparents on a great swath of land in western

Tennessee. His grandmother, a fierce woman who intimidated everybody, including her husband, was a big reader. She had books everywhere, and both grandparents read to Albert before he could read by himself. There was no school near their farm, so Albert was homeschooled for the first twelve years of his life. Grandma didn't have many children's books around, so she read him novels. Who knows how much Albert got out of Tolstoy, but he developed a great love of reading and a thirst for knowledge. Grandpa taught him to ride a horse at five, to navigate the boat across the river at six, and to hunt with a bow and arrow soon after. He grew up with a tremendous appreciation for books, literature, and music, and the outdoors. Albert carried this on with his children and grandchildren. Not surprisingly, his seven-year-old grandson is a good shot with a bow and arrow. He and Albert read together and explore the outdoors. Every minute that Albert spends with that little boy is a learning experience for them both.

Shannon is in her early forties and grew up in a small Iowa farm town. Both sets of grandparents lived there. They were farmers, so she learned the process of canning, and how to store the jars in the basement so you can easily find what you want. She learned to knit with one grandmother, and she read all the books she could find with the other grandmother. The big lesson Shannon tells me with a smile is this: in this farm community women are in charge. They run their homes and their towns, hands in the dishwater, aprons tied around their waists. The farm women set the tone of the town and bring the community together. The men may drive the tractors, but the women set the agenda. Imagine what spending all those hours in the loving company of a strong older woman does for a young woman's perspective on her life and on her future.

Agency

PARENTS STAND NEAR the slides in playgrounds, encouraging their children to climb the stairs and enjoy the ride down. All generations have a hand in encouraging their children to take a chance and master a new skill. Still, when a grandmother or grandpa urges you to do something on your own, to follow your dream, the message has a special salience. What's the difference between encouragement from parents and from grandparents? When the nonjudgmental sense of being accepted as you are—not as your parents want or as your peers require—radiates from the gaze of a grandparent, it's a confidence builder. Parents cannot always shed the cloud of worry from their brow. When a grandparent—who may have less investment in the outcome of your decisions, and who may know the real you better—offers words of encouragement the sky is the limit.

Vanessa and her brothers spent their weekends away from the city, at the farm of her step-grandparents. Oh, how she loved to be there. Her poppa was a salty old redneck who had as many strengths as he had quirks. One time at the farm, the family was watching a horror movie, something she wasn't allowed to see at home. Nevertheless she climbed into Poppa's lap and watched in his arms. She wasn't scared, and he gave her a cookie. "And you were mine from then on," he used to tell her.

This retired railroad worker loved breaking the rules. He used to take the grandkids on magic carpet rides. He'd take a tarp and put pillows on it, hitch the tarp to his pickup truck, and drive across the meadow. The kids would tumble off, and he'd turn the truck in a circle so they could clamber on again, and off they'd go.

Vanessa had a dream of being an actress. One weekend at the farm, Vanessa, by now a teenager, was in a poisonous mood. She'd had a big fight with her stepmother, and she stomped out to the pit where Poppa was tending the fire. "What's the matter, baby," he asked. "Nobody wants me to be an actress, nobody supports me," she complained. Then she saw him wave his hand and point his finger to the sky. "What are you doing, Poppa?" she asked. "Well maybe I'm writing it in the stars. One day, you're going to be a famous actress."

Now a graduate of Juilliard, Vanessa hopes to make her way onto the Broadway stage. There's no way to know what her career will be, but I know for sure that when she wins an award, she'll remember Poppa with his eyes on the stars.

Encouraging grandchildren to follow their dreams, despite the worries the other adults in their lives might harbor, is one of the pleasures of being a grandparent. We empower them when we bake together, garden together, write books together, teach them to knit and crochet, and stop cheating at cards to let them win as a nod to their becoming more grown up. We empower them in Grandpa's garage workshop when they hammer their first nail and saw their first piece of wood. Sometimes we let them see their own strengths even though we don't have a lesson plan.

Last winter I needed to help my colleagues stuff envelopes for a money-raising effort on behalf of a medical school and hospital diversity program. We had to get that New Year's letter out. My afternoon with my seven-year-old granddaughter was the only day my colleague was free to do this, so I took a chance. I told Ruby she was going to come with me and help stuff envelopes. She's scared of hospitals, so we walked carefully to the medical school offices and gathered in a quiet room. I had brought a book and a snack in case she got bored. She never got bored. She collated the pages for the envelopes we stuffed. My colleague and her sister were wonderful company. We had a ball. Ruby was proud of herself. She was doing something important for other people.

On a recent spring vacation, Ruby was asked what she wanted to do. "I want to volunteer for Hillary," she said. Now whatever your politics, seeing a seven-year-old at the computer making calls urging people to register to vote is a pretty great sight. Her father suggested that she introduce herself to people she reached by saying, "Hello, my name is Ruby and I'm seven years old." They didn't hang up. Nebraska went for the other candidate, but that didn't matter. She's now a political activist. Our time stuffing envelopes gave her a sense of her own power to change the world. The news of the election results, some months later, helped her learn that when we don't get our way, we find a path to go on.

Megan has daughters who spend many weekends at her in-laws' farm not far from their midwestern hometown. Grandma raises goats. The girls have been helping her around the barn for years, and they know more about goats than most of us. Last summer, Grandma had knee surgery, and the girls, now young teenagers, stayed at the farm for two weeks and took over Grandma's chores. You should see their stance, their shoulders, and the turn of their heads when they tell me about what they did, and how they took full responsibility at the farm. Agency? You bet. These kids do lots of important things with their parents, but the confidence they gained from the summer of the goats will help them stride into the world with straight spines.

Am I giving grandparents too much credit? Of course parents do the heavy lifting. But rounding off the corners of a child's character and strengthening that child's courage can benefit from more than one set of adults. And the joy of it is that we're not teaching, we're not preaching. We're just loving.

4

The More They Know, the Taller They Grow

....
The Impact of Family Stories
....

No, no! The adventures first, explanations take such a dreadful time.

—*Lewis Carroll*, Alice's Adventures in Wonderland

What do you remember about your grandparents? Were they fun to be around, or were they harsh and scary? Did they speak English? What was their mother tongue? Did they live nearby or far away? Did they get to know you? Did you get to know them? Were they immigrants striving to make a life for themselves and their families in a new land? Were they farmers eking out a living on their land? Woodsmen? Tailors? Teachers? Tradespeople? Postal workers? Cotton farmers? Bus drivers? Bankers? Stay-at-home moms? Children or grandchildren of freed slaves?

How many of their stories did you hear? And who told you? Today, piecing together the lives of our forebears is a national hobby. Some family constellations make it easier than others. Those of us who had immigrant grandparents perhaps couldn't cross the language barrier. We needed our parents to narrate the family history. Some of them did. Others stood silent. If you possess any objects—diaries, letters, pictures—that carry meaning, consider them the family jewels.

Our lives have touched at least five generations. In most families, that amounts to a century. History and people and events, joys and tragedies, happiness and craziness—all these elements are embraced in the generations that form our families:

Our grandparents, with their lives planted in the end of the nineteenth century and the start of the twentieth century.

Our parents, members of the Greatest Generation, many of whom lived through the Great Depression and World War II.

Most of us belong in some way to the baby boom generation, growing up during the greatest economic expansion in world history and being subject to the powerful dynamics that drove families apart.

Our children are the beneficiaries of all the stories we told them (even though they have forgotten most of them—they weren't listening).

> The grandchildren are growing up in a world
> transformed by globalism and technology.

With this perspective of the century in which we are embedded, we grandparents have the opportunity to enrich the lives of our grandchildren by acquainting them with all the generations we have known. We can become the griots of our family, the keepers of the stories and the tellers of the tales. Important messages about life, values, history, and perseverance are carried down the centuries through our voices. There's even psychological research that strengthens this point of view.

The Twenty Questions

CHILDREN ARE STRONGER and more self-reliant when they are nested in their family history, surrounded by information about their parents and grandparents, aunts, uncles, and cousins. This embedded information, researchers Marshall P. Duke and Robyn Fivush from Emory University have discovered, nurtures children emotionally and psychologically. These researchers report that children who are informed about their family history have higher self-esteem, a better sense of their capacity to control what happens to them, and lower levels of anxiety. These qualities turn out to be important for success in life.

The researchers devised the Do You Know Scale of Twenty Questions. It's important for a child to know where her parents grew up (questions two and three), where the parents went to school (questions eighteen and nineteen), and what jobs they had when they were young (question sixteen). Lest eager readers begin drilling their grandchildren about family facts, the authors are quick to point out that their twenty questions are representative of the knowledge kids get by talking with family members over time. Memorizing the answers is not the point.

The point is that children who grow up in families where there is lots of conversation are better grounded in their language and in their sense of autonomy. Even when parents are busy and stressed, and when the kids have their faces six inches from a screen, grandparents have stories to tell. Stories of the five generations carry different significance, and so it is important to be the carrier of all these tales.

Our Grandparents

I WAS NOT one of the lucky children who grew up with grandparents. They were all dead by the time I was born. But my mother had close women friends who were older than she. I attached to one of them, a master storyteller. We spent summers in her cottage on a small lake in Michigan. Mary, who was born in the late nineteenth century, told us bedtime stories as she, my brother, and I relaxed into the summer night on the screened-in porch where we three slept.

As a girl I pictured—and I still can—Mary as a girl riding on the back of a giant turtle on a beach in Florida where she grew up at the turn of the twentieth century. It was wild in the Florida she described, and the beaches went on forever. Giant turtles were plentiful, and they moved fast over the empty sand. The first time I got to Miami in the 1950s, I was horrified to see how built up it was. I had expected to walk on Mary's beaches and ride on the back of a giant turtle.

Mary traveled all over the world, even though she was a single woman. She told us stories of arriving in the Soviet Union soon after the Russian Revolution, of traveling by train through Nazi Germany in the late 1930s. My heart pounds as I picture her handing a Nazi officer her American passport. And the underlying plot of all these stories, one I only recognized as an adult, was that a woman alone could do anything, go anywhere, and make a good life.

Mary sang us songs from her childhood, and we did tongue twisters from an era long gone. Anybody know Theopholus Thistle, the Successful Thistle Sifter? My grandkids, born in the twenty-first century, do. Mister Thistle, the incredible tongue twister, has traveled from the nineteenth century to the twenty-first. I have taken many lessons from this pioneer woman. I wouldn't be who I am without her. Did she intend to form my character and courage? I don't know. But she succeeded.

To children born in the twenty-first century the circumstances of our grandparents are unimaginable. My late husband's grandmother was a girl in Kansas City when they shifted from gaslight to electricity—they turned on the lights. She told us how she and her family had walked down to the town square as dusk was falling. And then on signal, the electricity pulsed through new streetlights and suddenly the city was illuminated. When I remember Grandma Settie, I picture this scene. It's a tiny thing, but it's real because the story came from her.

When I tell a family story, I have no idea what effect it will have over time. Will he remember it? Does she care? Is it too sad? Too pointed? Does it have any point at all? Friends, it doesn't matter. The stories we tell enrich the fabric of their consciousness. My left arm reaches back a century as my right arm embraces my small grandchildren.

Who our grandparents were and how they lived sets the table for our family. I wondered what a random number of people remembered about grandparents, so on a lark I posted a question on my Facebook page, asking my baby boomer "friends" to tell me about the working lives of their grandparents. I was amazed to get over eighty replies, and together these threads create the tapestry of American history. Our grandparents worked hard to build lives, suffered tragedies of all sorts, and gave birth to the people who gave birth to us.

What charmed me and gave me fresh respect for the elder generation was the way in which so many Facebook friends answered my question and then went on to sketch the significance of the facts on their lives. Aesop wasn't the only storyteller to infuse lessons in the narrative. Jesus did a pretty good job of offering deep teachings in his parables, and so did the rabbis who created the Talmud. So when my friends related their grandparents' stories to their own lives, I realized again how character-forming these stories can be.

Claudia, a writer and editor, tells of her grandmother, a refugee who worked as a seamstress in New York City: "She went door to door on the Upper West Side, left cards, and did alterations for people. As a little girl, I went with her and carried her sewing kit. We'd sit in the living room while she fixed elegant dresses; I sat on the floor and made things with paper and glue." This beautiful story provided a metaphor for who Claudia became. "Today, I do something similar with words and images."

Others wrote of bread-baking grandmothers who fed family and hoboes through the Great Depression. Grandfathers who died young and others who survived the wars of the twentieth century, shoemakers and Communists—you'll find a model or a precedent for everything we are in the stories of our grandparents. I have a friend from high school whose grandmother always worked. Brought here from Russia in steerage, she married the love of her life, and they started building garages in the 1920s in Queens, New York. Grandma never stopped. Is it any wonder that my friend, who is closer to eighty than any other round number, still turns up in her office five days a week?

Our ancestors' stories contain tales of suicide, death, love, and sacrifice. They offered us, and through our own stories they offer our grandchildren, a sense of continuity and knowledge of the power within ourselves to overcome hardship and remain kind, generous, and hopeful. Adventure. Risk. Suffering. For many children raised in relative affluence in the twentieth century, hardship is a stranger. They're not hungry, and they're warmly dressed. Their homes are filled with stuff. Not so in the early decades of the twentieth century. The stories that my parents told of their childhood experiences gave me a mixture of pain and pride, and a profound sense of responsibility to put my gifts to good use.

When grandchildren hear these stories, they sift the sands of time for significance. Whether they are about work, struggles, heroic feats, or disappointments, these stories provide inspiration, curiosity, identification, and fascination.

Our Just-So Stories

IN OUR FAMILY, storytellers were prized. "You're a good raconteur" was high praise, and my mother was the best—she was the family griot. Were her tales, by the time I heard them, accurate? I suspect the edges were rounded (to make a good story), but they were true in essence. And they broke my heart.

My grandmother brought my six-month-old mother through Ellis Island in 1902. She was the family pioneer. Her husband would follow once she had set things up. She cared for my mother in a tenement on the Lower East Side and sewed pants, a penny a pair. They had no relatives here, so my grandmother did it all. My grandfather joined her six years later. By this time Rosie, my mother, was a sassy seven-year-old at the head of her class. She was the only one in the family, now reunited, who spoke or read English, and I suspect that her imperious personality showed itself to her father. He didn't like Rosie, and he beat her. Once he (mistakenly, he said, but she never believed him) spilled a pot of boiling water on her. She took refuge at the home of her best (and lifelong) friend, whose mother kept her skin cool long enough so there were no scars.

They were dirt poor, both parents sewing pants now. Rosie's mother kept getting pregnant, losing some babies while others survived. Being a smarty-pants, Rosie decided to read every book in the local library, from *A* to *Z*. Her father would beat her for coming home late, after the library closed. Later she attended an after-school social club for Jewish teenagers called the Uptown Talmud Torah. There she caught the eye of a young teacher, just a year older than she, who had skipped so many grades that he was graduating from college in his teens. He was editing the school newspaper, and instead of chief, they called him Cheese. He fell in love with Rosie Nadler, whose last name in Yiddish means "noodles," and for more than sixty years, Noodles and Cheese were together.

But in 1918 the flu epidemic hit Rosie's family, and both her parents died. Now Rosie had to take care of four little girls: the eldest was seven years her junior, and the baby was three years old. The stories of those years of poverty and sorrow were harrowing. I loved my aunts more than anybody in the world, and their childhood of suffering made me sad. Aunt Birdie, who was five years old when her parents died, often played hooky to sneak into local funeral parlors so she could weep among the strangers. She had been found screaming outside the doors of the emergency room, where she last saw her mother.

The stories showed me the centrality of family in the survival of our species, and they helped me understand my mother, who despite everything was an optimist. All her stories had a happy ending, no matter what pain they recounted. She made the immigrant experience my own. One day I went with a friend to Ellis Island. The main waiting room had replicas of the benches the immigrants sat on while they waited to be inspected and allowed into America. I looked down from the balcony and imagined my grandmother sitting there, my mother in her arms, and I wept. Now as I walk through Manhattan's Lower East Side, I have to use my imagination to see the world of my mother. But it's in my heart, and I hope to plant it in the hearts of my grandchildren.

So I tell my grandchildren about Rosie. They want to know how she survived, and how she coped with the hardships of her life. I connect these middle-class children with immigrants who walked the streets of the Lower East Side with holes in the soles of their shoes. The economic and social contrast between the elder generation and the youngest children is my message. It may not be the same for you. But you will find your own meaning and salience in the old tales you tell your grandchildren. And in the remembering and telling, you may understand something about your parents and yourself.

If you have trouble remembering much about that long-dead generation, there may be a book or a letter or an old photograph that spurs your memory. When she was doing research for her book about the Kennedy family, Doris Kearns Goodwin spent many hours talking with Rose Kennedy, who by then was very old and getting a little bit vague. Goodwin had been allowed to rummage through the attic of the house where Rose Kennedy lived. Every morning, before she began her talk with Rose, Goodwin would go to the attic and pick out some pictures or objects she thought might spark a memory. It worked like a charm. So if you have inherited anything from past generations, use them as memory aides when you retell the lives of your parents and their relatives. Let the grandchildren hold the vase, look at the picture, sit in the chair. Not only will these things spark your memories, they will make a strong impression on your grandchildren.

My mentor, Mary, collected jewelry when she traveled in Mexico. She let me play with the necklaces and earrings in the box that held them. Mary left the box to me, and now my youngest granddaughter rummages. When she's old enough, and she hears the stories I have told you about Mary's travels, perhaps they will have greater resonance because she has played with these relics for so many years.

Our Stories, Ourselves

WHEN WE HAVE exhausted the tales from the previous generations, we still have a trove from which to choose. I'm talking about our own lives. If you're old enough to be a grandparent, you've lived through times that children think of as history. What was it like to first see a color TV? Where were you when Sputnik went up? When John F. Kennedy was assassinated? When Nelson Mandela walked out of his prison in South Africa? When the first man landed on the moon? You can go on, and so can I. Kids love to hear our experiences and memories. Our lives are exotic gardens from which they can take sustenance. The words we speak and the tales we spin take them back in time and make the past come alive. We're not history books or TV documentaries. We're history come to life.

Here's an example. I was telling my grandson about what it was like to grow up in Washington, DC, during World War II. We lived across the street from an entrance to Walter Reed Hospital, and my aunts would take me to visit with the GIs who were resting on the benches or sunning in their wheelchairs. This was part of my war effort—smiling and chatting with wounded soldiers.

I explained that Washington at the time was a southern, segregated city. "No, Grandma," he said, "Washington was in the North. That's where Lincoln lived!" Centuries collapse for children. It is our job as griots to unpack history for them.

When we tell our stories, we have the opportunity to let them know that our lives were not perfect. It's important to tell them about our slips and slides, about our failures as well as our accomplishments. From their perspective, our ups and downs are shocking. But our strong responses may be heartening. My grandchildren know that I didn't get into my first choice of college, and how I suffered the night the letter of rejection arrived. That seems like a first world problem today, but I'm doing a little bit of resilience building for the times when they inevitably will be disappointed. My life is an open book for them, and it's not all roses. I'm not complaining, but letting them know about my ups and downs may relieve some of the pressure they feel to be perfect all the time. The banana peels we slipped on, the false starts, the disappointments, are part of our story—and theirs.

There's always the question about how far to go with grandchildren when we share our experiences. We don't want to burden them with our sorrows, but they have sorrows, too. It's easy to say to a child who has been excluded from a circle of friends that everybody goes through this. But if it turns out that you experienced a similar bad situation, feel free to tell the story. When we share these small moments, we cover our grandchildren in a protective context. Was she homesick at camp? If you were, too, say so. Does he have a terrible French teacher? Was he hurt by a friend? Tell him your story.

And then of course we did raise one of their parents. We have a whole lot of stories to tell.

When Daddy Was a Boy

HOW MUCH DO grandchildren love to hear tales of their parents when they were kids? We grandparents have those stories in our hearts and memories. There's nothing like the smile on a child's face when hearing about her father's antics—or her mother's bravery. I was fortunate to have a unique experience with my oldest grandchild. His uncle is the founder of StoryCorps, that great oral history archive. When he was eight years old this grandson, Benji, interviewed me. He dutifully downloaded a set of excellent questions from the Web site about who influenced me and what I hope my legacy will be, but those questions were asked and answered quickly. We had time left, so his mom suggested that I tell him about what his father was like as a kid.

The conversation began to bubble, with stories, and pranks, and silly shenanigans but also with important stories about what a fine person his dad was, even when he was young. We took that recording home and played it for the whole family. The room shone with warmth and love as we listened to the questions and answers. Luckily, that conversation rests in the Library of Congress, so Benji's grandchildren can play it for their children sometime in the twenty-second century. Technology will allow him to keep that, but it's an infinitesimal piece of our shared experience.

Every story we tell a grandchild about her parent as a child or teenager is a message in a bottle. Its significance goes beyond words. So when we think, "Isn't she just like her father," spell it out. Tell a story about how he made friends wherever he went, just like her. Our children were brave, and smart, and fun. Let the grandchildren know that. Sometimes they got into big trouble. The grandkids can know that, too. They will never forget these intimate stories about their parent. They will also remember the love that your voice conveyed in the telling.

On the Day You Were Born

KIDS LOVE HEARING about the day they were born. About all the cute things they did as babies and toddlers. At some young age, children forget their experience of being a small person. Think of Jane and Michael, the children in the Mary Poppins books who once could talk to the animals but as they grew up lost this ability.

All the stories we bored our friends with about our little darlings are perfect for telling again. It's impossible to recount them objectively, so filled as they are with love and amazement. The grandchildren see themselves through our eyes as thoroughly delicious individuals. It's one thing to say "I love you" to a child, but something else entirely to recall an early experience that may be different from the stories that have already entered the family lore.

The current vogue in child development is to focus on noncognitive skills: self-regulation, grit, and the ability to process stress. Loving attention from adults is essential to the development of these traits. Songs, games, playing, just hanging out, and of course stories all contribute to this. But the telling and retelling of these family stories have an additional benefit. The deeper the roots, the higher a tree can grow. We have the responsibility and the pleasure to give the new generation insight into where it came from, what every generation endured, how we slipped and fell—and picked ourselves up—and to spread their roots as far and as wide as we can.

5

Our Fountain of Youth

It is utterly false and cruelly arbitrary to put all
the play and learning into childhood, all the work
into middle age, and all the regrets into old age.
—*Margaret Mead*

There may have been a time when the pattern that Margaret Mead so vividly described was common. But that's not always true anymore. We live in an era when grandparents are connected across the generations. We can break down that rigid structure whenever we are together.

If we are still working, we know that we are headed toward the end of our careers. Some of us may be getting a whiff of regret that we are less engaged—and less ambitious. But when we sit on the floor and help to build towers of blocks, only to chortle when the toddler knocks them over, we travel back in time to the moments when our children were that young. Regret has no place here. When we make up silly rhymes with children or play make-believe with them, we enter our second (or is it third?) childhood—even if it takes a bit of concentration to get up from the floor, even if we need a nap after they have gone home.

This is the gift of the grandchildren. They keep us young. They give us the opportunity to play and to learn along with them. As we help them and their parents, with our love and time and support, we receive from them the strong possibility of better health and longer life. That's actually true. There's lots of research on this. A recent study published in the *American Journal of Men's Health* reports that grandfathers who are "involved" with their grandchildren are happier and less depressed. A recent ten-year follow-up study showed that the subjects who were not involved with the grandchildren died earlier than the Pop Pops who were engaged.

It's interesting to think about this. There's a mountain of research about attachment theory. The great psychologist and psychoanalyst Dr. John Bowlby introduced this concept to child development as a result of research on refugee children who had been torn away from their parents, to save their lives, and English children who were removed from their mothers during World War II during the Blitz in London. Bowlby argued that emotional and physical development happens as a result of the human attachments babies form with the adults who are with them regularly. Constancy is the goal. Without genuine attachment, babies don't thrive. Attachment theory, first promulgated in the 1960s, still offers sage advice for parents.

What about the grandpas? They crave attachment, too.

And if they're retired, or perhaps not so engaged in the world, the connection with grandchildren is a lifesaver. Attachment is a two-way street. Emotion flows both ways, and when it's positive, our bodies are bathed in enzymes that heal and make us stronger. Here are some of the reasons why we benefit so much from time with the children:

We get a chance to be silly again, even as we sag and creak. This is good for the spirit.

We get a second chance at being loving and attentive, when maybe we weren't able to do that the first time round. This is good for the soul.

We can heal our own wounds by doing for the grandkids what we missed ourselves. This is good for the heart.

We can stay relevant at a time when the larger culture begins to ignore us. This fills a gap in our lives.

We get a happier future to imagine, one that doesn't focus solely on walkers and canes.

Grandpa's Second Childhood

WE MAY PICTURE Grandpa sitting in the big chair reading the newspaper while the kids play on the floor, or we may think of the wise grandfather offering sage advice to children who may or may not be paying attention. But these days, men who did not play with their own children or act silly with them are now having a ball. Grandpas just want to have fun. I'm reminded of Lewis Carroll's "Father William" in *Through the Looking Glass:*

"You are old, Father William," the young man said,
"And your hair has become very white.
And yet you incessantly stand on your head.
Do you think at your age this is right?"

Paul, his wife, and I are sitting in the living room of a pleasant house in the Midwest. It's airy and full of light. We hear the sound of a car coming up the driveway, and Paul looks alert. He's in his midsixties, and, like many people of that generation, usually gets out of his chair a little slowly. But now he jumps up and runs out of the living room. "Something must be up," I think. The car stops, the doors open and slam shut, and in walks a four-year-old boy. Actually, he doesn't quite walk in. He sneaks into the house. He comes through the door and crouches. His blue eyes narrow, and his expression reminds me of a cat on the prowl. "Hi, Grandma," he says to my friend. But he doesn't stop for her. He's looking for someone.

Then, from behind a couch at the end of the room comes a sound. "YAAAAAH." Paul bounds to the little boy, and picks him up for a hug. Then he puts him down and disappears again. The hunt for Grandpa continues. This hide-and-seek lasts for a few more minutes, with extended hunts, howls of laughter, and several YAAAAAHs. This ritual is how Grandpa greets his grandson whenever he arrives. Who is the youngster in this picture? Of course it's the little boy, but the grandfather is behaving like a kid and having a fine time.

Paul is not alone. Larry, a retired management consultant, spends two days a week with his grandchildren. He's another Father William from a different stanza:

> "You are old," said the youth, "as I mentioned before,
> And have grown most uncommonly fat;
> Yet you turned a back-somersault in at the door—
> Pray, what is the reason of that?"

This is what happens when Larry arrives at his son's house to watch the two grandkids:

"When we first get there, if I see their parents are busy doing something, I grab a couple of their stuffed animals and a big horse and start doing my make-believe thing. They immediately grab one and they follow me, and then we jump on the bed and we say, 'OK, let's pretend this is a boat,' or ship, or whatever, and they're totally into it—I'm saying it's a matter of a minute, from when I walked in the door."

Larry isn't turning somersaults, but he is completely into this game with the boys. The plot of their make-believe takes unexpected turns and involves every room. It used to be fairy tales and now it's superheroes. Who knows what it will be tomorrow? The kids never stop in the middle of the game and say they're tired and ready to watch TV.

Larry loves this, but after a while he wants to read the newspaper. He does that for a while. "Quit reading," they say. And it's back to make-believe. They stop the silliness over time, then talk, play games, go outside, eat lunch, nap, and so forth. Larry still mentors young executives on the rise, but the purpose of his life is these children. "My grandchildren are one of the major reasons why I am so wholly comfortable and at ease in living, because they are the joy of my life."

Other grandpas I have spoken with echo Larry's sentiments. People who don't have the experience (yet) say to him, "Are you crazy, Larry? You're babysitting two days a week?" Larry tells me, "And I look at them and I say, 'Are you kidding? This is the highlight of my week!'"

The physical benefits of being with grandchildren also include a lowered risk of Alzheimer's, researchers have found. We don't know enough about the causality of depression or the aging brain to understand the mechanisms of this benefit. Part of it must be that grandkids allow grandparents to recover what it's like to be young again. All those happy feelings flood the brain with good chemicals.

I was surprised and delighted to meet so many grandfathers who embrace their new roles. It's less of a surprise to see grandmothers laughing and dancing with the grandkids. But like all elders, we grandmothers need permission to behave like kids.

I live a block away from the place where all the trains traveling into Grand Central Station go underground. You can watch as the trains come down the track and then disappear into the tunnel. You can see them erupt onto the track as they head north and then fade into the distance.

There's a little tiny park right there, which I named Choo Choo Park. My grandchildren and I would sit and wait for the trains to come and go. You could spot two tiny circles of light far away, and then watch them gradually, slowly, get larger. Suddenly, a train races down the track and in a flash disappears into the tunnel.

We could get closer to the trains by standing on the sidewalk above the tracks so we could see where the trains came in (there's a fence to keep you from falling onto the tracks). I realized that if I danced around, waved my arms, and shouted, sometimes the conductor would notice and give us a good toot toot. Oh, the joy of being able, in my fourth quarter, to feel free to dance and wave my arms on a New York sidewalk (without fear of being taken away).

Some years later, I was passing Choo Choo Park as I walked my dog, and I saw a gray-haired woman waving her hands and jumping up and down as the train neared the tunnel. I looked again. Yes, of course, right next to her I saw a younger woman with a little boy in her arms. See? I'm not alone.

Remember the children's zoos where adults can't get in without a child? Our situation as elders reminds me of that sign: NO ADULTS ADMITTED WITHOUT A CHILD. Being silly is a powerful antidote to the rigors of age. Get your grandchildren and let the silliness begin.

A Second Chance

IF YOU ARE a person who has no regrets about how you behaved with your children (the parents of your grand-kids), feel free to skip this section. But if by chance the rigors of your life and work didn't allow you the time or energy to give your kids all that you wished you could, or if the circumstances of your life mitigated your enjoyment of their childhood, you're in for a treat.

Ruth's husband was a tough father, full of rules and judgment. His daughters knew he loved them, but play was not his forte. Ruth tells me that sometimes she thought of him as a petty despot. His way was the only way, and the girls were afraid of him. Imagine their astonishment when they had children. This tough man became Paw-Paw. Silly, loving, even risk taking. He bought the grand-kids a trampoline, and after they mastered the basics, he would take out the garden hose, water the trampoline down, and add liquid soap. The grandkids jumped, slid, and threw themselves around in the mountain of bubbles they created. Suddenly, this kind of playfulness came easily to Paw-Paw. When his second chance came around, he grabbed it.

Robin, a successful businesswoman, has two children under two and a full-time job. Her mother, who had not been particularly engaged with Robin when she was a girl, moved nearby to help. She loved those babies and gave them the attention that Robin never felt she got from her mother. Over the years the old distance, the old sorrow dissipated. Robin's mother died before I got to ask her if this was intentional. But Robin and her kids' memories of this woman are deeply ingrained. "She gave my children what she never could give me." That epitaph describes the second chances that grandparents sometimes get.

Grandparents have plenty of time and patience, which expands and enriches the moments. I'm not alone in regretting that I didn't have the leisure to sit and watch the grass grow with my kids. It's not just because I worked. All mothers are besieged with tasks to do. There is never enough time. As grandparents we can relax with the grandkids and enjoy the moments we so rarely had with our kids.

My younger grandson was a train nut at six and seven. My house at the beach is near the train tracks. You never know when a train will arrive, and waiting takes patience. One summer weekend, Tobey was dying to go see the trains. As we left the house, it started to sprinkle, so we went back and got jackets, then back to the tracks.

"Train in the rain," we sang on the way. We walked under trees as much as we could. It was heaven for the boy. We inspected the tracks, we looked at the gully on the side of the railroad, he noticed the broken concrete near us, and we stood a minute under the tree, which kept us dry. It began to rain harder. We started to walk home. "Train in the rain . . ."

Then Tobey stopped. His hearing is better than mine. "I hear the train." We turned around. Then I heard the train, and we walked a bit closer. He smelled the train, and then we saw the train. This boy was beside himself, and so was I. This whole event took maybe twenty minutes but our time together expanded immeasurably because of the tiny moments we shared.

How to Stop the Disappearing Act

AS BABY BOOM grandparents retire, many of us have a sense of being put aside, of no longer carrying power or authority. Work is the first to go. While many consider retirement to be a boon, some boomers miss the purposefulness that work provides and the status that comes with it. For some, retirement can feel like a demotion.

This long-term disappearing act is gradual. I work out twice a week, and my posture is excellent. I try to walk like someone decades younger than me. But when I've had a long day, my shoulders fold forward. My long stride turns into short steps. I hold on to the staircase rail as I climb the stairs slowly and huffily. I can regain my youth after a good night's sleep, but when I feel old, I fade. There is a natural way to fend this off: grandchildren.

Picture the smile on the face of a little one who shouts, "Grandma!" Small children run and grab our legs, and then as they grow they grab our middles. Later, we get a regular hug. That greeting is habit forming. It comes whether or not we bear gifts, and it comes if we see them regularly or infrequently. The kids help to repair our loss of relevance.

...

Henry, who is a retired professor, considers the years when his grandsons were young to have been the best years of his life. Henry took early retirement from his university teaching job. His hi-tech specialty was an area where progress was happening at Mach 1 speed. He felt that he couldn't keep up with his younger colleagues, and if he couldn't be at the top of his game, he didn't want to play. He and his wife live near his son's family. They were available to babysit and be with the children for years, so when Henry retired, those boys filled in the gaps. "I didn't have to think of, what will I do to enrich my life? I had them."

Henry's wife was still teaching school when the boys were small, so Henry picked them up at school and took them to the park. Henry instilled in them a lifelong love of a local baseball team (the Cubbies). The kids' school knew to call Henry when one of the kids had an accident and went to the emergency room. "I have many things that I thought I'd want to do, but they filled up the void. They made those seventeen years fantastic."

Now Henry's wife suffers from dementia, and she spends the days in an eldercare facility. The boys are grown, and they don't visit as often. But he still lights up when one of them texts and asks to come over for a meal or a visit.

Over the last decades, Virginia has lost multiple identities. Her husband was a famous writer, whose death left a hole in the literary world and in her heart. Virginia went from courageous partner to keeper of the flame. When she sold the business she had founded in order to support the family, Virginia lost another aspect of her identity. But there was a remedy. Along came the grandchildren.

She readily took on a new role: Grandma. Virginia, who had worked when her kids were small, began to babysit regularly—and with pleasure. She held birthday parties in her home, hosted Sunday suppers, and had graduation parties in her backyard. She made friends with their friends. She was a haven when the grandkids needed her.

Virginia worried that when they grew up, they would disappear from her life. It wasn't easy for her to watch as one after another of the former babies, toddlers, teenagers, graduated from high school. She accompanied each of them to college for the first time, and she would always come home just a little droopy. Since there were five of them born over the course of a decade, someone was always at home. Then the inevitable happened: the youngest got into college. It was a blow. What would she do without him?

Time came to the rescue. Many of the older grandchildren are building their lives. Now they turn up, or get in touch, not from necessity but for the pleasure of her company. They call her for advice. She doesn't have special expertise, but she's smart and they know she's looking out for them. The grandkids have kept Virginia relevant for the last quarter of a century. She doesn't know where she would be without them.

…

If the grandkids help to make us feel important, there's something else they do for us: they see us through the lens of love. Sheila tells me about an offhand conversation she had with her teenage granddaughter:

"Grandma, you're beautiful," the granddaughter remarked as she looked up from the computer to greet her. Sheila has always been self-conscious about her weight and was surprised to hear this. Sheila shook her head and muttered, "Well, uhh." "No, people don't see it," her granddaughter said, "and they don't see it because they don't want to see it, but you are." And then she turned right around and got back online. Sheila sits up a little straighter as she tells me about this moment. And she looks thrilled. She is beautiful. Just old enough to look like a grandmother. Women's eNews reported on a survey of women over seventy: they are more concerned about losing their memory than losing their looks. Sheila might agree.

Healing Old Wounds

A SPECIAL KIND of healing can take place when grandparents are good to their grandchildren. Sometimes we get to do for them what was never done for us.

One winter I spent three days with my grandson. His nasty cough had turned into walking pneumonia, the babysitter was sick, and I was between gigs. It's not really babysitting, with an eleven-year-old. It's a chance to lounge around, chat, read, nap, check facts on Google, or ask Siri stupid questions. On the second day, his mother offered to find someone else to stay with him. "No," I said, "I can do this. I have the time, and I love it. I'm not going to have this kind of time with him forever. He's growing up, and he'll get busy." Those days stand in my memory wreathed in sunlight.

But there's more to this story than Grandma spending quiet days with a boy. It's about my childhood. My mother was a busy woman. She wrote a daily column for a New York newspaper, and she worked at home. She didn't get dressed until she went out at night. Bed jacket on her shoulders, yellow legal pad on her lap, pencil in her hand—wisdom flowing from her brain.

Her childhood was full of tragedy. Orphaned at the age of seventeen, she raised her four little sisters single-handedly. One of them, her favorite, died young of rheumatic heart disease long before I was born. The death left its mark. My mother couldn't listen to classical music because Blanche played the piano, and she couldn't bear to enter a sickroom, because Blanche had died at home.

So my mother rarely came into my room when I was sick. When I was thirteen, I had a bad case of mono and was in bed for six weeks. She was working in her bedroom and never entered mine. My dad, who worked from his home office, stopped in between patients, but I was alone the rest of the time. Once an aunt came to visit. She sat in my room and read the paper. She did not talk much, but it was such a relief from my loneliness.

The days I spent with Benji when he was not feeling well meant that I was also doing for him what wasn't done for me. We were healing together.

The Gift of a Future

HAVE YOU NOTICED that we as grandparents age less rapidly than babies and young children grow? If I try hard, I can take myself back in time and recall the vigor of my step the day my first grandchild was born over a decade ago, but the changes in him are so much more dramatic. He's gone from an infant into a teenager. And I just need a nap some days.

When I turned seventy-five a few years ago, I welcomed what I called my fourth quarter. In good health, with the energy of a younger person, I concluded that seventy-five is the new something. But I wondered how much of the lives of my grandchildren I would live to see.

This worry had landed on me one spring day before that summer birthday. I was on my way to pick up a grandchild at her school, a short walk from Columbia University. On this May afternoon, as I walked up Broadway, the sidewalk was filled with new graduates and their families. It was commencement day. I was elated to see so many trios moving down the street, parents on either side of the floating graduate, gray-blue robes billowing in the sunlight. I nodded and smiled a look of congratulation to each family. Joy and pride mingled with just a bit of relief, I thought.

Then, without warning, I began to weep. I wouldn't live to see my grandchildren graduate from college. I'd need to be in my middle eighties for that. I can feel the tears behind my eyes as I write this. I wanted to stroll down a campus street with my graduating grandchild, remembering the first time I held that baby, and all the moments from that day up to the graduation ceremony. That walk up Broadway haunted me. I comforted myself with the thought of Grandparents Day, perhaps an elementary graduation, perhaps a bar mitzvah, or even a high school graduation. Who knows?

Then I discovered some heartening statistics. Grandparents are living longer. More young people have living grandparents at their college graduations and even at their weddings. If you get to be seventy-five, you have a good chance you'll be around for another decade. This prediction is based on probabilities, and if illness strikes, those numbers can rear up and smack you in the face. But still, there's a chance, a good chance of living to a greater age than we ever expected.

One night in January I woke up with a start. In my sleep I realized that this is the year my passport expires. I never thought I would outlive the expiration date. My mother died at the age I am now. Emboldened by this new data, I decided not only to renew my passport, but also to request extra visa pages so I can go wherever I want. Silly? Confident? Maybe the numbers are in my favor.

I don't worry about looking older, and I am only slightly resentful when strangers call me "Sweetie." I don't mind it when younger neighbors ask me, "How are you doing?" in that syrupy concerned voice. I used to watch with fear and pity as elders made their way in my neighborhood with canes and walkers. Now I don't. We're getting older, and if we can still navigate the city streets, if we can still get where we need to go when we want, then bravo to us.

Survival is for something now. It's to be able to see our grandkids become who they are meant to be. It's to participate in the real life of the next generation. So what if the bones ache, the hearing aids eat up batteries. Grandchildren help us to picture the future—their future, and ours. Canes? Walkers? Wheelchairs? There's a song we elder grandparents get to sing to ourselves, as the grandchildren grow up, go to college, move out of the house, and even marry. Remember the title? "Get Me to the Church on Time," from *My Fair Lady*.

PART III

Real Issues, Real Solutions

6

Love and Sacrifice

I love Mommy, but I don't like her.
—*Christopher, raised by his grandparents*

Imagine a large raft floating down a river. It's a family excursion. Everybody is there. Three generations watch the riverbank slide by. They talk, the grandchildren play, perhaps some adult puts a hand in the water to feel the current. They drift in peace.

Suddenly the river loses its placidity. The raft roils. Have they hit a rock in the river? The parents are in trouble. Who will save the baby? Grandma dives in and swims the child to safety. The youngster is rescued but needs care. Somebody has to step up. Guess who?

The Dream of Retirement Deferred

WHEN ELEANOR AND her husband learned that they were going to become grandparents, Eleanor in a flash offered to care for the infant until she was old enough for day care. I have heard from many grandmothers about their days spent tending the new baby. It's exhausting but a labor of love that is only possible if you live nearby or can be away from home for those months. This makes it possible for the baby's parents to get back to work without worrying about leaving the infant with strangers. Grandparents get a chance to be embedded in the life of that child. Eleanor was happy to step up.

She had a wonderful time, and when Annabel went into day care, Eleanor took her all afternoon, until one of the parents came home. When Annabel was in grammar school, Eleanor ferried her to music lessons, to soccer games, and sometimes out to a lovely splurge at the local ice cream shop. Eleanor and her husband had put off their dream retirement: volunteering in third world countries for months at a time. But they knew that Annabel would be more self-sufficient in time.

So far, this family's raft had been floating smoothly down the river. Then, when Annabel was in third grade, her parents informed Eleanor and her husband that they were getting divorced. Annabel would travel back and forth between her mother's and her father's houses. She could bring the cat with her wherever she slept.

So Eleanor, on the spur of the moment, made a promise:

not only would she continue the after-school program, but she would also take care of Annabel on school vacations and holidays. "Just send me the school calendar," she said, "and I'll put it in my schedule." Eleanor's husband was surprised at this offer. Later, when they were home, she explained the strategy behind her offer. Yes, it meant putting off the travel years, but Annabel's mother, a top Silicon Valley executive, could leave town for a better job, anytime she wanted. She could take Annabel with her, and the family would lose the everyday company of their darling granddaughter. Eleanor figured that free and year-round babysitting services would be an incentive for her daughter-in-law to stay in town. She was right.

Eleanor was happy to fulfill her promise. Her husband, not so much. Those early years after retirement are times of good health and energy, but he was eager to have them pack their bags and set out for what might very well be their last adventure.

Adding to the angst in the household was her husband's disappointment with their son. Why couldn't he keep his marriage together? They didn't try hard enough, he thought. They should have stuck it out, he believed. Eleanor's husband was unhappy with the sudden change in plans, and Eleanor didn't enjoy her life in the middle, between her husband's wishes and what was good for Annabel.

It would have been easier for the family if Eleanor's husband were happier with her decision, but everybody survived. Annabel, now in junior high school, doesn't need them, and this couple is still well enough to enjoy the rigors of eco-travel around the world. Now, they send postcards, which suffice. They weathered some rough patches, but compared to many grandparents, they are extremely lucky.

The decision to put off retirement, to deal again with potty training and the school system, is not simple or fun. But when the parents are incapable of caring for their child, the choice is to keep a grandchild in the family or to put the child up for adoption or into the foster care system. Today more than ever, in large part because of the opioid epidemic, grandparents become caregivers again. What keeps these grandparents going is their love for the child and their determination in the face of serious problems to make sure he or she thrives. Even though they are tackling all the responsibilities—and frustrations—of parenthood, they don't lose the grandparent glow when they talk about the child. It's a good thing. The difficulties and pressures put on these grandparents are monumental.

When there's enough trouble in the family that Grandma becomes Mama, shame creeps in. And so does the judgment of strangers. Financial sacrifices are part of it. Fatigue and stress are constant companions. Exhaustion. Anxiety. Anger. Jealous siblings and anxious spouses complicate the situation. And then there's the little one who asks, "Who is my mama? Where is she?"

Millions of grandparents find ways to cope and raise the grandchildren. It's far from easy. With minimal support from the government or the community, it is a long and demanding journey. Still, custodial grandparents take strength from their knowledge that they are protecting the grandchild from the welfare system and from a chancy hope for the kindness of strangers. They do their best to provide safe and stable homes. They hope the grandchildren will always carry the sense of being loved. And they feel they are doing their best to ensure their grandchildren don't lose connection with the rest of their family—aunts, uncles, and cousins.

Sometimes It's Almost Too Hard

SHARON IS A pioneer in the world of caregiving grandparents. Over twenty years ago, long before the heroin and oxycodone epidemic hit the middle-class white community with unrelenting force, she and her husband took over the care of their grandson. Looking back at the decades when they cared for Christopher, Sharon remains furious at the daughter who abandoned her baby, but she and her husband are proud of how well Christopher has done.

Christopher was an adorable child. Bragging about him twenty years later, Sharon tells me how he taught himself to read at three and figured out how to tell time on a real clock by the age of four. He was brilliant. Christopher could fix anything that was broken and had an early affinity with computers.

The trouble is that he wasn't so good at being toilet trained or at doing what he was told, but at first Sharon and her husband attributed it to his age. He's just a little one, she and her husband thought. He'll grow out of this. He was also charming, so charming that he could talk his way out of trouble. As Christopher grew up, being able to concentrate and to do what he was told were not his strengths.

Then Christopher developed serious behavioral problems. A big kid who grew into a large young man, Christopher became nearly impossible to control. Sharon would call the police just to help her get Christopher to do what they needed. Sharon tells me that over the years she became best friends with the school psychologist, and then with anybody in authority who could help her grandson. When the public schools stopped working for Christopher, Sharon and her husband found schools that could handle him. He never graduated from high school, but, like many computer whizzes, he did fine. Not having a high school or a college degree has not so far stopped him from making a life.

Sharon attributes Christopher's ADHD to being exposed to drugs in utero. We're not sure what hard drugs do to the fetus, but we know it's not good. Sharon's daughter experimented with drugs when she was a teenager, and by the time she reached her twenties they became the focus of her life. Like so many adolescents with this affliction, she dropped out of school, stole from her family, and was eventually kicked out of the house.

She disappeared, and they lost contact. Then the call came: "I've just given birth." Sharon and her husband rushed to the hospital to meet their grandson. Their daughter came home with her baby, and they both attended the hospital's detox program. Just about two years later, something changed. Sharon can't put her finger on it, but the day her daughter said she had to go on an errand to a neighboring town, Sharon suspected something was up. She worried, but she couldn't stop her from leaving. Christopher's mother reassured her son that she'd be back that night and gave him a big hug and kiss as she left. This toddler stood by the window all afternoon and evening, and until Sharon and her husband put him to bed. He stayed at the window the next morning, and for the rest of the day. For weeks he asked for his mother.

Gradually the fact that Mommy wasn't coming back sunk in. Occasionally she would turn up at home, mainly seeking money from her parents. She would pour affection and warmth on the boy, and then she'd disappear. One year she promised to visit for Mother's Day. Christopher and his grandfather carefully picked out a card, which Christopher decorated. They waited on the sofa for his mother. At the end of the day, when he realized that she was not coming, Christopher apologized to Grandpa: "I'm sorry I made you waste your money on a card."

It was hard on Sharon and her husband, of course. But they understood that this was the behavior of people who were addicted to hard drugs. It was much harder on Christopher, who couldn't understand what he had done to send his mother away.

The final blow came when Christopher was ten years old. His mother had been released from jail. She arrived with a surprise: a brother and sister for Christopher, a set of twins who had been born in prison. She was raising these children, and she thought it would be good to visit regularly. The only thing was, she would be taking the twins home with her and leaving Christopher with his grandparents. Sharon worried about the toll these visits would take on Christopher. She wouldn't subject her grandson to serial abandonment. So she refused to make Sharon's visits with the twins a regular part of their lives.

Christopher's mother eventually did get off drugs, but she still can't get a decent job and lives on welfare. She keeps on asking Sharon for money. The last time she visited the house, Sharon's daughter disappeared upstairs for a few minutes. When unusual charges appeared on Sharon's extra credit cards, she realized what her daughter had been doing upstairs—stealing the cards. Sharon is more than fed up. She has done enough. She believes that twenty years dedicated to Christopher should suffice.

Mother and daughter sometimes get together for lunch, but they wind up arguing. Sharon can't understand why her daughter was so irresponsible and never put her baby first. Her daughter replies that she made a wise decision— she left her son with the best possible parents. Both women are right.

Sharon and her husband took on the care of their grandson without support systems, except Sharon's energy and determination. That was over twenty years ago. Since then, grandparents raising grandchildren have become more common and better understood. Resources to help them are still minimal, but in a similar situation, Joyce and her husband found a rich array of help for themselves and for their grandson.

Making the Best of a Tough Situation

ON HER WAY home from work, Joyce picks up Tim at day care. Some days her husband does that job. At home, husband and wife telegraph their day to one another while they give the five-year-old his snack and settle him down with his tablet. The adults trade off making dinner and all three sit at the table together. After dinner they go outside and play sports until everybody is ready to drop. Then Tim takes his bath and jumps into bed. This looks like a typical day in an ordinary family, except that Joyce is sixty-one, and Tim is her grandson.

Joyce has several things going for her. She's got her energy, a husband who agrees with the plan, and her faith community. She and her husband also have a fine fallback: their therapist. When their disagreements disrupt the relationship, off they go.

Lori, their adopted daughter, had a history of mental illness, some stemming from a brain injury when she was a teenager, and some from some traumas she experienced later in life. As she grew up, Lori became obsessed with finding her birth mother. She went on the quest with her boyfriend. They disappeared for several months, and when they turned up, they were married and Lori was pregnant. After the baby arrived, the new family moved in with Joyce and her husband. All was calm for a while until the husband became violent with Lori. Exit husband. Eventually, things settled down enough for Joyce and her husband to take a short vacation, leaving Lori and the baby at home.

When they returned, there was no Lori, no baby, and no information about their whereabouts. Then they eventually learned that Lori was working as a desk clerk at a crummy motel in another state. She and her infant lived in a squatter with no running water or electricity. When Lori discovered spiders crawling over the child, she drove home and dropped him off with his grandparents. Tim, now five, has been with Joyce and her husband ever since.

Joyce loves that little boy, who is adorable, if a little headstrong. She's not sure if his behavior is normal, because she raised only girls. And she has lingering worries about his mental health, considering his volatile mother and her problems. So far, so good, but there are issues. They have to do with Joyce's daughter.

Mother and daughter are estranged. Like many custodial grandmothers, Joyce is furious at her daughter and protective of her grandson. She doesn't want him to be around his mother. She worries that he won't know where he belongs. He's not old enough to understand why he doesn't live with Mommy. "When I was in your tummy, Grandma," he begins. She corrects him. "You were in your mother's tummy." "Did I have my trucks there?"

Her husband disagrees. He has more patience for Lori, and he thinks Tim should know his mother. Over Joyce's objections, he takes Tim to visit his mother several Sundays a month. Joyce worries that these visits will leave Tim confused and conflicted.

Experts tend to agree with Joyce's husband, although they suggest that grandparents be sensitive to how much— or little—children can understand about the situation, depending on how old they are. Tim's questions are evidence for Joyce's point of view. On the other hand, how can you keep a mother away from her child, even though you can't depend on her? This is the kind of conflict that Joyce and her husband take to the therapist.

Despite all this, Joyce has support from many areas of her life. She and her husband are dedicated church members. They aren't the only grandparents in the congregation who are raising grandkids, and so they don't feel judged or isolated. They feel embraced. When they gained custody of Tim, the pastor threw them a shower. One friend gave them a year's membership in a local pool. Another offered day care one weekend afternoon a month. Tim wakes up Sunday morning eager for church. He loves it there.

Joyce has her health. She's a young sixty-five, and she's not as exhausted as other grandmothers seem to be—even after a much shorter visit. Maybe her strength has built up gradually over the years of taking care of Tim. Joyce and her husband have put off any thought of retiring when they expected to. Their two incomes suffice. Tim so far has shown no disabilities, and if he continues to be the sweet and smart little boy he is today, they needn't worry about his behavior in the future. And they have a great fallback. Tim's aunt and her husband have offered to care for this boy if something happens to them. Though Joyce and her husband have custody of their grandson, they are also considering adopting him, so that he will inherit their Social Security and health benefits.

Joyce and her husband are stable and loving people with

a (generally) harmonious relationship. That forms the bedrock of Tim's security. They work together to make the best of all possible childhoods for the little boy, and he benefits from their thoughtful care.

What if that isn't the case? How does the grandchild who is raised by grandparents who aren't quite as stable, who has traveled around the country hiding from her biological mother, and who has seen some pretty harsh stuff grow up? Well, here's Carrie, full of energy, rage, and a thirst for stability and a good life.

No Good Deed Goes Unpunished

CARRIE IS TWENTY-FIVE years old. She is a smart and well-put-together young woman. She has a profession, a loving boyfriend, and a future. She was brought up by her grandparents (although her grandfather was rarely present). There's vinegar in her voice when she tells me that her parents conceived her in a flophouse where people bedded down after a "rainbow gathering." They were both high on acid. The only reason she's in this world today, Carrie tells me, is because her mother had a drug-induced dream of a curly-headed little girl running through a pasture and decided not to abort her (Carrie was her mother's fifth pregnancy—the others had been terminated).

Carrie's childhood memories are dominated by a single image: looking out the window at the front yard waiting for her birth mother to come home. Like many children who have been left to their grandparents, Carrie remem-

bers a childhood full of longing and rejection: "Longing,
like the front half of you is cut off and it's somewhere
else." Carrie's birth mother left without telling her family that she wasn't coming back. That's how Carrie landed
with her grandmother, the woman she now calls Mother
(but with an edge), and with her then husband, whom
Carrie calls Dad.

Carrie will have nothing to do with her birth mother.
She sees her as a predator, a woman who harms and takes
advantage of everyone in her path. Carrie's voice turns
hard when she describes her birth parents. They never
married, and her birth father disappeared before Carrie
was born. She says that her birth mom was the abuser
who has been in and out of jail, rehab, and in and out of
Carrie's life. When she was eighteen, Carrie met her birth
father. They spent a couple of weeks getting to know each
other, but there was no connection, and then he left town.
It was too late for them both.

Carrie's grandmother was afraid that her daughter
would stay clean for long enough to claim Carrie and take
her away. One year that fear became so strong that the
whole family moved to another state to live with Carrie's
aunt. They changed their last name for the time and were
virtually in hiding. It was about then that Mother decided
to get custody. She didn't want any more close encounters.
Carrie isn't sure if she was ever adopted, but that's moot,
now that she is an adult, on her own, and lives thousands
of miles away.

Carrie is clear about her birth mother, the predator, but
she is profoundly ambivalent about Mother. She was the

only constant element in Carrie's life. She loves her and is grateful, but she carries a weight of anger and resentment toward the woman who cared for her and raised her. She admits that she was a resentful and uncooperative teenager when she lived with Mother and Dad. Now she understands why Mother was the object of her childish rage—Mother was the only stable element in Carrie's life. Still, with the perspective of her quarter century, Carrie doesn't understand why her grandmother is so accepting of her wayward adult children. Mother has five grown children, four of whom are in trouble. Carrie is furious when Mother lets them into her house and allows them to steal, cheat, and impoverish her. Carrie doesn't have the status or resources to help her grandmother, and she feels powerless. Some of Carrie's gratitude has bled into sorrow.

Carrie is a survivor. She realizes how fortunate she is. She credits a series of self-help programs she enrolled in and benefitted from. If it weren't for them, who knows where she would be? She's been through the gamut of programs, from mind-body exercises to Al-Anon, from yoga to nutritional cures. Getting clear and staying strong are so important to this woman that she will not stop seeking and growing—probably for the rest of her life.

Carrie's resilience sends a message to grandparents who are raising their grandchildren:

Born to an addicted mother? Yes, but she's overcome the deficits.

Brought up in a chaotic setting? Serially abandoned by her mother? Sure, but she thrived.

Is she conflicted about the woman who cared for her?
That comes with the territory.

Is she contemptuous of the woman who abandoned
her? Yes, but Carrie's resilience has helped her find
ways to grow.

Like a plant turning toward the sun, Carrie finds
sustenance where she can.

The Unbidden Angels

CARRIE KNOWS WHAT Mother did for her, and she realizes the sacrifices her grandparents made on her behalf.
Tim is too young for gratitude, so that gratitude lies with
Joyce and her husband, who know how fortunate they are,
compared to the situation other custodial grandparents
face.

What these grandparents do is to love and care for
their abandoned grandchild. They aren't young anymore,
and many don't have sufficient financial and emotional
resources. But they muddle through, and with all the
sorrow, with all the sacrifice, they are grateful for these
children. Perhaps they take comfort in the fact that they
may be able to give the grandchildren a grounded and
loving start in life.

For much of the twentieth century, when there was a
troubled child or teenager, we blamed the family, especially the mother. Blame and guilt form the two-headed
monster that accompanies behavior that deviates from the

norm. It's an especially heavy burden for grandparents who care for and bring up their grandchildren. They blame themselves for the behaviors of their addicted or wayward child. Then they blame this adult child for relinquishing responsibility and placing the burden of the baby onto them.

In addition, grandparents worry that their grandchild's development will be in some way hampered by the exigencies of birth or by neglect. Taking the blame as they take the responsibility adds to their stress. Unlike Joyce and her husband, many grandparents don't talk about the circumstances that brought the child into their home and don't reach out for clinical support. And as the *Hechinger Report* points out, "When grandparents do look to their friends for support, their peers are more likely to be empty nesters, no longer able to relate to the challenges of raising children." Perhaps now that the opioid epidemic is making headlines, grandparents will get some help, and perhaps they can talk with others who share their circumstances.

Grandparents who are raising grandchildren are heroes, even if they are imperfect caretakers. Their actions join a tradition that stretches back into human history. It's called kinship. It requires putting the well-being of the weakest first. Most grandparents with whom I have talked don't complain about their sacrifice. They recognize what they have given up over the years, but when they speak of the grandchild, their voices turn buttery with love. Anger is there—especially at the grown child whose poor decisions landed the baby in their home. Disruption is there. They have lost years of easy life, and many have to put off retirement. But once they dived into the river and grabbed that child, they had no choice but to rescue it and take the consequences of their decision.

7

Staying Close While Living Far Away

An increasing number of grandparents choose to relocate in order to live close to their grandchildren, the *New York Times* reports. Picking up and moving to be near the grandchildren may be the ultimate solution to the space-time puzzle, but it's not for everybody. And it's far from a simple decision. This chapter is about all the ways grandparents can solve the distance puzzle—short of relocation.

Children don't experience time and space the way adults do. They live in the moment. That's why parents are wise not to tell about the impending arrival of a sibling until the pregnancy is well along. A little one can't imagine what six months means. And we have all experienced the child in the backseat of the car who interminably asks, "Are we there yet?" The child doesn't mean to be annoying. It's just that periods of time don't carry concrete meaning for children.

I was visiting my granddaughter Ruby's second-grade classroom. After we were done with the program, we had some time to chat. I asked Ruby's friend about her grandparents. She adores them. Where do they live? "Grammy and Grampy live down the street. My other grandparents live in LA." "Who are you closer to?" I asked. She shook her head in confusion. "I love them all." "What do you do with the grandparents who live nearby?" "I go there most afternoons, with my sister. We play and we bake and have dinner." "And your California grandparents?" "We go to Disneyland," she said with a triumphant smile.

Jessica's paternal grandparents were divorced, and they lived a thousand miles away from her and her mother. She visited them once a year. Grandpa picked her up at the airport and kept her for a few days. Then he handed her over to Grandma.

Jessica went with her grandpa on his business rounds. He sold carpet to theaters and churches. The visit with the nuns was her favorite. The nuns loved this little Jewish rug man, and he adored them. He was proud of his granddaughter, and the nuns doted. They always kept a carved wooden animal or two—mainly ducks—for her, so she would sit in the corner and play with them. Jessica gets that faraway look of happiness when she tells me this story.

Her grandmother, on the other hand, was a celebrity hound who lived in Beverly Hills. They went to the movies together, sometimes two a day, and they loved spotting all the movie stars. Jessica is now a tenured professor who hides her celebrity magazines in her desk drawer. It's still a fun part of her life, thanks to Grandma.

These stories offer consolation to grandparents who do not see their grandchildren very often. Children usually cherish the time they spend with their grandparents, no matter how much, and they never forget the adventures, the tastes, and the smells. Adults are the people who fret about time between visits and the miles apart. We have a pretty good sense of time and space, and for many of us, distance is painful. Our dimension of time includes the reality that the grandchildren won't be young forever, and we are getting older.

Keeping up a vibrant relationship with grandkids who live far away takes effort, planning, and often money. And it evokes in us a wide range of our strong emotions. We miss them when we are absent. We treasure our time together, and we feel a loss when we part. And don't forget the complex array of feelings, positive and negative, that we share with our grown children. That's why I propose the three *P*'s: Patience, Perseverance, and Perspective.

These three P's are especially useful when you're in the family cauldron, where there are lots of people, old relationships and new ones swirling around. With all these caveats in mind, here's a list of the strategies families use to solve the space-time puzzle. Grandparents often choose from this menu:

We use modern technology to create a real connection. Screens work.

We think up ways to lure the family to visit us at home.

Retired, or semiretired, we visit our far-off families as time and money allow.

We adopt a policy of taking each grandchild, alone, on a trip.

We invite grandchildren to stay with us for long periods of time.

We take family vacations, yearly or when the opportunity arises.

Gramp's on Screen!

PAULETTE JILES'S WONDERFUL novel *News of the World* tells the story of an elderly man living in the nineteenth century who was a news reader. He traveled by horseback or in a covered wagon through Texas, gathering clippings from newspapers and from wire services, collecting a hall full of people, and reading them news and articles from all over. He charged a dime for the evening performance. People had no other methods of learning what was going on. Letters from home took months, and events around the world could pass unnoticed.

Today we are fortunate to be in touch instantaneously. As I write now I know that in a few years technology will have made another leap or two. But the fundamentals remain relevant—unless some genius invents space-time travel.

First and foremost, find a way to communicate that suits the child. Small ones sometimes have trouble talking on the telephone because they can't picture the person on the other end of the line. So Skype might be better. Experiment to find what they enjoy.

Samantha lives on the East Coast and has parents in Australia. She began FaceTiming with them when the baby was in his high chair. They called home every morning at breakfast (which was evening Down Under). She tells me that an early verbal request from this baby was "See Papa?" Screens are part of the children's world. When it comes to keeping up with the grandkids, don't worry about the impact of this screen time on their growing brains. The impact of singing "Itsy Bitsy Spider" with Grandpa, screen to screen, is undeniably just fine.

Some older kids don't like screen time. So they may prefer to text. That seems to be today's preferred manner of communicating with the young. Our grandchildren have a shockingly easy time with technology. It's good to let them teach us. We will learn, and they will be proud educators.

Melissa is one of three sisters, and her first child was also a girl. Then she had a son. Melissa's mother and father were perplexed. They didn't know how to deal with a boy. It showed when they visited, and Josh was hurt. Why didn't Grandma and Grandpa pay him attention? Why didn't they engage him in conversation? When Josh was ten years old his grandmother's computer went on the fritz. Enter Josh. He fixed it, to her delight. Then he taught her how to text on her phone. They have discovered a new way to "talk." And then, to everybody's delight, Josh introduced his PhD-in-literature grandmother to emojis. She loves them. Go know, as my friend Jo Ann says.

Julie, her five sisters, and their parents live thousands of miles apart, so they have created a family photo stream on their smartphones. They post snapshots all the time as a way to connect. So when Julie's toddler asks to see his grandparents, aunts, uncles, and cousins, it only takes a second for him to catch up with the family. We used to say that a picture is worth a thousand words. Julie and her sisters get that. Kids love pictures of the family. Keeping up-to-date in this way is a vigorous antidote to distance.

Those smartphones also make it easy to send little movies. If there's a favorite book you read to a grandchild and you miss each other, get somebody to film you reading that book, and send it along. Marilyn is reading the Harry Potter books with her faraway granddaughter on FaceTime. If you're going to be away for a long time, make a little movie of yourself singing a bedtime song and send it off.

Notes to grandparents: We look awful on the screen. Don't worry. We look wonderful to the children.

It's smart to be sensitive to the method of communication the grandchild prefers. If it's a phone, fine. If it's e-mail, that's excellent, and if it's texts, terrific. Don't expect a response from a grandchild on a device he or she doesn't use. I know one grandfather who was furious with his grandson for not returning his e-mails. It took a visit home for him to learn that nobody under twenty-five reads e-mails—it's all texting today, and who knows what tomorrow.

How to Lure Them Back Home, and Why

WHEN MY SONS were small, we lived in New Haven, ninety minutes by car from my parents. They wanted us to visit, although they were old and didn't have the staying power we now expect of ourselves. Still, my kids loved their visits. In my day, we were fiercely aware of something called "overstimulation." Do you remember that? Keep them calm. Don't get them too excited. My mother, who knew a lot, thoroughly ignored that concept when we visited. She wanted to be exciting, and she was. They sang and they danced, and by the end of the weekend the kids were definitely overstimulated—and exhausted.

Sunday afternoons we would pack the boys in the backseat and head home. The baby would cry, and later the two boys would fight all the way to the Dewey Thruway. Overstimulated? You bet. Exhausted? Oh, yes. Then they would fall into a deep sleep and be refreshed by the time we got them home.

When Kimberly and her husband had their first child,

they were a two-career couple worn out by the end of the week and ready to settle in at home. Her in-laws lived several hours' drive away. The effort to pack everything up and to drive so far with the baby daunted them. But her husband's parents were clever: they outfitted a nursery for the baby, with all the stuff that a baby needs, including sufficient changes of clothing to last the weekend. And her mother-in-law did the baby laundry to prepare for their next visit. They had the right toys for the little boy as he grew up. They furnished their backyard with swings and climbing things. My friend and her husband threw a change of underwear in the car, took snacks for the ride, and off they went—regularly. It was easy, and of course their little boy—and the brother who followed—begged to visit Grammy and Gramps every weekend.

Having a backyard, these grandparents were able to enjoy some quiet moments of rest when the kids were outside. Access to the outdoors offered a salve to the family tensions that naturally arose. Weekend visits have the great advantage of not allowing enough time for meltdowns, tantrums, arguments, and the like.

Families separated by more than a few hours' drive face other obstacles. If there's a flight involved, going through security lines with small children is a nightmare. So a weekend doesn't always make sense, and the visits get longer—perhaps over a holiday. But when the visit stretches out to more than three or four days, the atmosphere can get tense. Not simply between the grandchildren and the grandparents, but between the two adult generations. Grown children, no matter how old, can be drawn into childhood family disputes. They regress, and so do we— we're suddenly back in the trenches.

In addition to these tensions, families face disagreements about how the grandchildren should behave, what they should eat, and how they should be disciplined. Formal people expect table manners, for instance, and parents too busy to sit down with their children for a meal may not have taught them to sit still until the last bite is swallowed. Children today spend more time on screen devices than some grandparents think is appropriate. But if the grandparents interfere with the family ways, there can be trouble. On the other hand, if television and sugar are prohibited at the grandkids' home, lenient grandparents can cause eruptions. Accidents happen: children fall down and hurt themselves, and valuables fall down and break.

Here's a tip: when things get tense, get out of the house. Use the children as an excuse for a getaway, which is the best treatment for tension. Consider a visit to a park, or museum, or a playing field. Then there's the matter of babysitting. If the grandparents are trusted enough to be alone with the grandchildren, there's an easy exit for the parents: a movie, a dinner, or an hour spent with old friends. It's a way to reduce the pressure and have some time alone. I offer only one caveat: when parents get back to the house, the kids may have splurged on ice cream, may have watched nonstop TV, and may still be up, dancing some wild dance with Grandma. Parents: grin and bear it. The silliness across generations does immense good. You'll be back to your sugar- and TV-free environment in no time.

Setting Boundaries on Silver Lake

HOPE AND HER husband live across the country from the grandchildren. They bought a small cabin on a lake near where the grandchildren and their mothers live year-round. And because they are retired, Hope and her husband spend summers there. They call it Silver Lake Camp, and they have fun every day. Hope's Facebook posts all summer are filled with pictures of trips, art projects, animal friends, and shared classes. I was in awe of Hope, and a little jealous, because I imagined that she could last all day, all summer with the three little girls. When we caught up with each other in person, I discovered her secret: a four-hour maximum. When the four hours each day are over, the kids go home. I'm actually more in awe of Hope now, because she has figured out how to maximize her time with the children and minimize the stress on herself and her husband. They babysit to let the mothers have some peaceful time, and they have weekends to themselves, for their own work and relaxation.

It's not just the cottage that impresses me, and it's not

the natural beauty of the lake. It's the boundaries they have set and conversations they have shared—in order to make Silver Lake Camp a place of fun and comfort.

Am I a Houseguest or a Hostage?

MANY GRANDPARENTS VISIT their faraway families when they can. That's what frequent flyer miles are all about. Zoe has three grown children and three grandchildren, spread across the country. I sometimes wonder how she and her husband can bear to spend endless hours on TSA lines, but they have no choice. How else would they get to spend time with the grandchildren? They adore those kids, and they'll put up with long lines and uncomfortable flights. They will also put up with tensions in the homes of their grown children.

Emily visited their prickly son. There often were hard moments when the son would take after his father in hurtful ways. The big old house could hold them all physically, but not the emotions that swirled around the adults. So they found a solution: the Airbnb down the street. Now, when tensions are about to boil over, they claim fatigue and head out of the house. Everybody decompresses and things cool down. Gloria never stays with her grown son and his wife. She takes a hotel room and brings the grandkids to stay with her. It's a treat for everybody.

The grandchildren we visit don't always cooperate. They have busy lives, even when they are four or five, and they don't always want to drop everything to spend time with us. Have you ever come into a room and greeted a grandchild who is on her iPhone? "Hi, Grandma," she mutters as she looks up. Then she looks down again. This is painful. After all, we traveled all those hours and miles, spent all that money, and still we don't get their attention. *P* for patience works here. Eventually the excitement of that phone will wane, and the little girl will be ready for a chat or a story.

Then there's the looming possibility of a fight between the adults. Random comments can be hurtful. It's hard to be thick-skinned when we're tired and out of our comfort zone. I'm a pacifist when it comes to everyday conflict with the grown children. Peace in our time makes it possible to form the bond with grandchildren. That connection will outlast the conflicts that we experience. It's what we call *perseverance*.

For some grandparents, being stashed in a grown child's house is unnerving. As we get older, we like our privacy. Do you really want to share the bathroom with your daughter and son-in-law? And what about the sleeping arrangements? Sofa beds can be a little hard on aging backs. We put up with the discomfort for the pleasure of being with the grandchildren. But picturing the quiet and comfort of being home is allowed.

Other grandparents are not bothered by the odd sleeping arrangements and by the changes they endure. Norma is not given to understatement. "I love it," she says of her visits. "They come in my bedroom, they wake me up. I've never been so happy in any relationships as I've been with these grandchildren, ever." This San Franciscan has one family in Texas and one family in Maine. What about all that travel? "I told my boyfriend I'm not even interested in traveling anymore. I'll go to Texas, then I'll go to Portland, then I'll go to Texas, then I'll go to Portland. Do we need to see Paris again? I'm not sure."

And she doesn't even get along so well with one of the daughters-in-law. Since she doesn't drive, she is marooned at the Texas house. That just means she takes good books to read or a pile of crossword puzzles and waits for the kids to get home from school. The tensions between these adults worked themselves out over time. What is the balm in Gilead? The grandchildren, and how much they love their grandma.

The best trick, of course, is to get the grandchildren away from their parents. They behave better when they are alone. Everybody knows this. Perhaps it's the unwavering gaze of love they experience. Perhaps they are so enmeshed with their parents that they keep up their old habits when they are together. Perhaps it's just that they want us to love them—and we do.

So, get them alone.

It takes some ingenuity to figure out how to spend time with each of the grandkids alone when you're visiting the whole family. Take a walk with each of them or play a special game. Like all enduring bonds, this bond is created one-on-one. Think of it as an emotional umbilical cord, through which flows love and affection. It flows both ways and nourishes both generations.

Camp Gran

SANDY LIVED SEVERAL hours' drive from her daughter and the granddaughters. She had a full-time job and couldn't take off whenever she wanted to. Her visits to the grandchildren were sporadic. The girls greeted her with a whoop of joy and a running hug. But there wasn't enough time together. So when she retired, Sandy founded Camp Gran. Sometimes the camp is on the move, and sometimes it stays put. She planned to spend a month in France one summer with a ten-year-old granddaughter, but she was too young, and the trip was too long. After two weeks, the little girl got homesick and Sandy got the flu, so they went home early.

Then Camp Gran became a week-at-a-time event. The younger granddaughter, who now is a political activist, was into art, so for a week she and Sandy took in every museum they could visit in New York City. The granddaughter fell in love with the Greek painted pottery at the Metropolitan Museum of Art. Sandy sat on a bench and brought a magazine to read while her granddaughter inspected every pot. There are a lot of pots at the Met.

Things don't always go smoothly on these trips. Once Sandy and a teenage granddaughter got lost in the old section of Grenada, Spain. Grandma failed at her Google maps job, and the teenager got furious. She marched off—into the unknown. Sandy was frightened because they didn't have a phone connection. A fifteen-year-old girl with no Spanish was wandering through backstreets in summer shorts. Sandy returned to the hotel and began to fret. As the hours went on, she got a little angry. But the worry and anger vanished in relief when her granddaughter arrived at the hotel, delighted with her adventure.

Then came the year she took another adolescent granddaughter to Montreal. It's a lovely city, and they had fun, but the teenager wanted green hair. Really green, and her parents were opposed. Still, at Camp Gran anything goes, so they found some green hairspray, which they applied in the airport ladies' room (after they had gone through security), and emerged from the gate to greet the parents— green hair and all. It washed out easily.

Sandy is now a little bit older, and Camp Gran has migrated to her house on the shore. Last year she was scheduled for major surgery and asked that somebody come and stay with her during her post-op recovery. The Girl with Green Hair volunteered. They spent most of Sandy's ten-day recovery in Sandy's big bed, napping and watching junky TV. Camp Gran is also good for Grandma.

I don't have the time or the resources for long trips. But I have taken the older grandkids away overnight, by train, to nearby cities, and it's fun. The very fact that this is her time, or his, makes the difference. I let them choose what they want to eat, where they want to go, and what to do. It doesn't matter to me. The time together is what it's all about.

The Staycation

AN EASIER AND cheaper version of Camp Gran is the staycation. Taking each of the grandchildren home for a few days seems challenging at the outset, but many people find it easier and more fun than they expected. These visits can begin as soon as the child is ready to sleep away from the parents for more than a night. I have friends who take each of the grandkids for a week to their home in Minnesota. There's plenty of room, these people saved the best of the toys from their children's childhoods, and there's always the nearby ice cream shop. Their five-year-old granddaughter behaved more like an adult than she ever did at home. She arrived with a suitcase, which she unpacked neatly in the dresser in her room. She was so well behaved. When she began to wilt and feel homesick, off they went to the ice cream shop. Another ice-cream cone or Popsicle wouldn't kill her.

Her older brother, who can be a bit willful, is an angel in Minnesota. He will eat what they serve (not so much at home), he finds ways to amuse himself, and he has the ability to calm himself down. He loves working in the garage with his grandfather, and he's a big reader, so a trip to the town bookstore is his version of the ice cream shop. These kids come home with improved manners, but of course the improvement isn't permanent. Why should we expect it? When they're home with their parents, they revert to their habitual selves.

When grandchildren are old enough to stay with out-of-town grandparents, they can also survive a bit of un-orthodox behavior, such as:

Cold pizza for breakfast

Unlimited screen time, to give the grandparents a break

Staying up very, very late

Spending a whole day in pj's

Dinner in bed watching TV

Dessert first

Riding in the back of grandpa's pickup truck

Using power tools in the workshop

This is a short list. You can add to it. Breaking the rules gently with older grandkids and doing what they want (within limits) is fun on occasion. But don't get lured into thinking that what happens at Granny's stays at Granny's. If the grandkids want the same privileges at home, they'll snitch. So be mindful of the parents' deep wishes even as you bend the rules.

There's also the list of things they get to do with us that their parents may not have the time for:

Playing old board games

Going to the town dump

Exploring new woods or lakes

Visiting the historical society

Learning new gardening skills

Cooking a lot, and baking another batch of cookies

The Great Family Gathering

I KNOW A man who considers the annual trip with his wife's family an "obli-cation." He grumbles about it, but he also enjoys it. It means a lot for him to see his children together with their cousins. The relationships among cousins are special. These are close relatives without the stress of sibling relationships. When the cousins are together, they are like bits of metal near a big magnet. When they get older they may put on a skit or invent a tradition. Hosting such a gathering may be exhausting (also expensive) for the grandparents. But being there to see the next generation form family bonds is an antidote to the sorrows we may carry.

Grandkids climbing the walls, adult siblings watching who gets how many potato chips. Cousins loving one another one moment and fighting the next. What am I talking about? You know. It's the great family gathering. Be warned, they are complicated, sometimes frustrating, and often out of control. It's best to just relax and let it happen. Plenty of unstructured time, very few instructions, and a laissez-faire attitude keep things rolling along smoothly.

The Power of Ritual

ANN IS ONE of six siblings. She comes from a big Irish family. Each of her parents had ten sisters and brothers. Imagine the crowd of cousins. Her great-grandmother, the matriarch of the family, was a talented lace maker from the time she was a girl. She would protect her fingers with gloves, so that scratches or cuts wouldn't impede the making of the lace. Those clever fingers got her to America, and they helped her support her eleven children. They share three large articles of faith: profound love of the Catholic Church, a deep patriotism for this country, and an everlasting belief in the importance of the family.

For decades, the family has met at a resort not too far away from where they live. It's a place with skiing, snowboarding, and it has an indoor pool. Long tables in the dining room hold the family at meals. Their weekend is Presidents' Weekend. Ann tells me that soon after they put away the Christmas decorations the children start making lists of what to take to Longberry. Swimsuits, skis, board games, you name it. Then with the advent of great-grandchildren, Longberry had to make room for fifty-eight relatives.

And then the number went down to fifty-seven. Ann's twenty-five-year-old daughter died suddenly. Ann talks about it years later, and I can hear the sorrow that lies behind her matter-of-fact voice. To commemorate Elle's life, the next year the cousins pooled their money and bought a plaque to name a Longberry park bench in her honor. Now, soon after they arrive, they all walk together to visit Elle's bench. One year they gave all the little girl cousins manicures. Elle loved to dress up. The following year, all the little girls paraded to Elle's bench as angels.

If you get together somewhere every year at the same time, that trip punctuates the lives of the children. I take my children and their children away for a long weekend every winter. It started out with my two sons and their wives and one toddler, and now there are nine. Years ago, my grandson Tobey named it The Nine of Us, and so we remain. It's always a huge effort, and at first I felt as if I were negotiating a nuclear arms control treaty to find the time and the place that everybody agreed on. But over the years, the rhythm of the long weekend overrides the complexities. The grandchildren create their own rituals and look forward to the trip all year. As everybody gets older, busier, and more engaged in school life, it gets harder to plan. But we'll do it as long as we can. The Nine of Us—that means a lot.

In a recent conversation about my will, one of my sons suggested that I create a little fund so that they can afford to continue the winter trip after I'm gone. The Eight of Them? Why the hell not? I'll be there somehow, just as Elle is present when her family visits Longberry.

8

Who Gets What and When?

My late husband's grandmother, who lived a good ninety-four years, had many grandchildren and great-grandchildren. She wanted to give them each a birthday check, but there was no way she could remember all the dates. So Grandma Settie made up her own system: she sent each of us a check on her birthday. What a good idea. We still celebrate this generous and feisty woman. And we never forget her birthday.

Molly's grandfather lived with his daughter and her husband—and their five children. Pops would watch the children at the town pool all summer, and he always had a dime for a treat—for each of them. I'd been wondering how Pops could afford to be so generous. Then I realized that ten cents for each child amounted to half a dollar. That wasn't much in the 1960s. But it felt like a fortune to the children. These gifts from grandparent to grandchild are memorable.

Aside from the holiday gifts and the family visits, which are bound to the traditions many of us share, we are faced with the reality that our families are under the pressure of limited time (two-career families) or of insufficient funds (the static standard of living). Since our generation of baby boomers benefitted in large part from the economic expansion of the second half of the twentieth century, many of us are in better financial shape than our kids. And if we are retired, we have time.

So how do we spend it? How do we balance the varying needs of our families with our own needs? We want to be responsible—and loving—parents and grandparents. But the questions of allocation are confusing, and the answers are not always simple.

For grandparents to come up with the mixture of generosity and fairness that's right for each of the children and their families is not easy. We consider our resources and how we want to use them. We think about the varying needs of our different families. We can't make these decisions in a vacuum. Spouses don't always agree about how to spend their later years and what to do with money—if there is any.

It's so complicated. And then things change. A grown child may lose a job, a grandchild becomes sick. The stock market takes a plunge, or a divorce puts new pressure on a family. A lucky child gets a generous stock bonus when her company is sold. A sibling decides to dedicate her life to a cause whose rewards are ethical, not financial. The childless son thinks that he is shorted of gifts and support because he doesn't have children.

Some grown children treasure the fact that they are self-sufficient; others treat their parents like an ATM machine. Some don't need or want babysitting help; others act as if the grandparents have nothing else to do. Is there a moment when you Just Say No, in the words of a former first lady? How do you encourage independence while still helping when you can?

There are too many unknown variables to be able to solve the puzzle of time and money. But I have a job here, and that's to help clarify your reality, your values, and your hopes and dreams for the family. This is the great balancing act of grandparents. It makes for conflict, and it keeps changing. It keeps us limber, and with luck, it offers all of us the chance to think and then communicate, to be generous and to receive gratitude. Our first task is to take stock. Consider these questions:

What are our resources?

How do we make decisions about how to use them?

What about fairness and competition between the grown children and grandkids?

How much do we reveal to our grown children about our own needs and our resources?

How do we imagine our true legacy?

...

You might think that the hard part is figuring this all out. Well, even more challenging is communicating to our grown kids what we are thinking about the present and the future. If we can have a conversation with them, hard as that is to contemplate, our balancing act will be easier in the long run. The danger of misunderstandings, or disappointment, or arguments, or even a serious fight is scary. Think about what you might say to your grown children as you read these pages. Remember that the best medicine for misunderstanding is conversation. And nothing breeds misunderstanding faster than the allocation of time and money.

Time Is of the Essence

I WAS LUCKY to have as a great friend and teacher a rabbi who was a human rights crusader and a wise man. Marshall Meyer created many aphorisms. One of my favorites is this: "People say time is money, but they're wrong. When you run out of money, you're poor. But when you run out of time, you're dead."

So the first question is: How do we spend the time we have left? Do the grandchildren come first, or do we have our own work to do, other passions to follow? What are our obligations, and what are our dreams? Do they correspond to the needs of our families?

Working grandparents don't have much time to babysit

and linger the way retired grandparents do. Some still have elderly parents (or other relatives) who need help. Elder parents often take priority because the need is so great. So they are stuck in a triple-decker life: call it the Club Sandwich Generation. There are only twenty-four hours in the day. Not having the free time to spend with the grandchildren can be misunderstood, especially when our families watch other grandparents pick up the kids at school and take them to the playground. Where's Grandma? Where's Grandpa? Every grandparent has a different answer.

Grandparents who live far from the children and grandchildren have the problem of distance, and that's another puzzle to solve. We can't be there to pick up the kids at school or camp, but at least our absence is not automatically construed as a lack of attention or love.

The Granny Culture is everywhere, on Facebook and in the blogs. These virtual grandparents seem spectacular, and they take great pleasure in showing how generous they are with their time and attention. This culture puts pressure on busy grandparents to be everything to all the grandchildren, everywhere they are needed, and at all times. However we present ourselves, divinely happy or terribly harried, the truth of our situation is complicated. "Perfect" grandparents get just as tired and stressed as the rest of us. They just don't admit it—in public. In our hearts we may believe that it's unfair to demand perfection from anybody. But that's the situation many of us face. It sets an impossible standard and gives regular grandparents a complex.

In response to this atmosphere, my Alabama friends tell me they are terrible grandparents. "I don't change diapers," they say. (Even though they have taken their daughter and her husband and baby into their home and are supporting them.)

I met a successful Dallas career woman who says, in a defiant tone of voice, "I don't babysit!" Then she admits that when her daughter has a crisis, she'll drop everything to be with the child. What this busy executive means is that her daughter needs to deal with day care on her own and can't depend on her to be the Granny Nanny.

Even so, it's hard to set limits on the requests for time and energy without feeling guilt or appearing to be selfish.

While it may appear that the "right" way is to drop everything for the grown children and the grandkids, it's not always the case. That's why it is so important to take stock of how much time we have, and how we want to spend it—and then, with trepidation, find a tactful way to communicate it to our children.

"It Takes Two to Tango." Remember that song? It's true for couples. They have choices to make—together. If they are retired and considering relocating, is it right to move to a sunny place to play golf and be with friends? If they are idealists, how do they choose between being a volunteer in a third world country for months, or doing a round-robin set of family visits? These are important questions, and disagreements can erupt. Compromise is hard. But on the other hand, if a couple has survived together long enough to have grandchildren, this cannot be the first conflict they ever faced. People in their second and third marriages may not have spent so many years dealing with conflict. But the reality of blended families offers its own set of problems—and solutions.

When Bryn decided to keep her daughter's baby until she was old enough for day care, her husband, a proud grandpa, didn't object. He was still working, and the fact that his wife was so completely occupied was fine with him. By the time he retired and was ready to move permanently to the Southwest, a place with the weather of his dreams, Bryn and her granddaughter were so embedded in each other's lives that Bryn wasn't ready to move. Her daughter by this time had divorced and was struggling as a single mother. Grandpa was not a happy camper, but the difficulty of his daughter's situation won the day, at least until the little girl was old enough not to need Grammy. Now she and her husband are out and about, enjoying the retirement they dreamed of.

Tina's mother still hasn't retired, although she began receiving Social Security more than a decade ago. Tina is resentful that her mother fills her day with projects, attends art classes and lectures, and visits galleries in cities all over the world. If an interesting trip coincides with a grandchild's birthday, she will send a card and leave a gift, but she's not about to cancel her plans. If Grandma is in the middle of a project and Tina suggests a surprise visit to the studio with the grandchildren, Tina's mom may be sorry to miss out on the visit, but if she's busy she tells Tina that she doesn't want to be interrupted. Tina thinks her mother is selfish and doesn't love the grandchildren. Many of Tina's friends' parents—the ones who have plenty of time—drop what they are doing at a moment's notice: they are "good" grandparents. Of course Tina's mother loves her daughters and the grandchildren, just in her own way. She will visit with them when she finds it convenient.

Tina's mother has always been engaged in her career and passions. Perhaps Tina dreamed that she would be more attentive to her grandchildren than she was to Tina and her sisters, but her mother stayed true to form. Tina never had to deal with a mother whose happiness depended solely on her and the grandchildren, so she lacks a basis of comparison. Still, as Tina's children grow up, she notices how much her children love their busy grandma, and how much they enjoy their time with her. The oldest daughter is now in college, and she calls her grandma to report on her classes. So Tina's mother can be an adviser and role model to her granddaughter. How is that not a good thing?

I ran into such a conflict last summer. My Manhattan children invited me to spend a weekend with them in the country. They had been away on vacation, and we missed each other. But my book deadline loomed, and I wanted to make it a day trip so I could wake up at home on Sunday and get to work first thing. Of course I loved being invited, but I had a job to do.

"Can't you stay over?" my son asked. "We can all have breakfast in the morning." I had to say no several times before they accepted my decision and drove me to the train station. Their feelings were hurt, and I felt bad. Was I making a mistake? What was I thinking? The next day, my son sent me a text, making sure I got home safely. Then: "BTW we were talking this morning about how proud we are about your commitment to the book. You are so purposeful. It's inspiring." Whew.

This generation of grandparents is younger and healthier, and many of us are fully engaged in our own interests. We play golf and bridge and we travel. A higher proportion of elders are doing volunteer work than ever before. We enroll in adult education courses. We participate in church activities, volunteer in schools and hospitals, and do all sorts of exciting and rewarding work. In the long run, this is good for us and for society.

When there's a crisis, all bets and interests are off. Gina, a woman with many grandchildren and a busy life, dropped everything to help her daughter when the twins came way too early. These were teacup babies, and they needed constant feeding and changing, 24/7. So Gina stayed with her daughter and took one of the three shifts, sleeping when she wasn't on duty. She lost track of day and night, and remembers these six weeks only hazily. The twins are now four years old, and those tough days are forgotten. Her other grandchildren did without her help until the twins were older and safer.

Sometimes, as in this case, grandparents have to focus attention on one family over another. Kim's parents were planning to move to her town to help with the children. But then Kim's brother and his wife had a child with a disability, and Grandma was needed there. Kim was glad that her mother had the stamina to help her brother's child.

Long Division

GROWN CHILDREN HAVE an inborn app that counts the time and attention they receive from parents and automatically compares that to what their siblings get. That app, which I think of as iMischief, came into being long before computers (think of Cain and Abel). It's a simple translation app that turns commonplace decisions into lasting judgments.

Saying no means: I don't care for you (or perhaps your children).

Yes means: I love you.

Suggesting a cut in the amount of babysitting means: your kids are getting on my nerves.

Being slow to take up on an offer to do something expensive with grandchildren means: they don't matter so much to me.

Looking just a little annoyed at some grandchild's
antics means: you think we are bad parents.

And, tragically, going overboard with praise means:
what are you really thinking?

If we grandparents want peace in our time, and easy relationships with our children, we need to disable this app.
And there's a very good method for doing that. It's called
conversation.

It's no secret that the remedy for misunderstanding is
communication. We need to tell our grown children what
we are doing, when, and why. Of course it's hard to begin
such a conversation, and we never know where it will end.
So bring up the subject while you're in the car, or cooking.
Or on a walk. Talk about what's going on, about what you
are thinking, and how you are dealing with the situation
at hand. Disagreement is possible, but so is resolution.
And as parents and grandparents, we have a right to be
respected for our decisions. It helps if our reasoning is
clear and we are making an attempt to be fair.

One of the overwhelming tasks we parents have is to help
our grown children see us as ordinary people who love
them, but who no longer have superpowers. That's another
reason why it's good to spell out exactly what's going on.
The more they know about what's happening with us, the
weaker that troublemaking app will become.

We have an obligation to give our children and grand-children an understanding of our notion of a life well lived. We do it best by living our life well, according to what matters to us. That's our legacy. If Grandpa is a quiet man, who doesn't engage much in the family scrum, but finds a way to listen to his grandson like no other person can, he's teaching a lifelong lesson about quiet and noisy. Grandma's passions sometimes make her a subject of family laughter: How could you be so excited about what the dog did? Maybe it's not important, but children learn that they can enjoy silly and small things to the limit. Grandchildren watch how we deal with the exigencies of our lives, the situations that take us away from them: illness, loss, and troubles of all kinds. We give them models, when we want to and even when we aren't thinking about it.

Thinking about Money

IT'S A HARD subject. Money carries multiple meanings: love, approval, judgment, dependence, and rejection—for starters. It's hard to figure out how to be generous and fair at the same time. What is enough? How do we secure our financial future and also help children and grandchildren in need? How do we choose between a family vacation and the money for a new roof or boiler? Do we spend down our savings in an emergency and then pray we don't live too long?

...

A little history offers perspective. Our parents, the generation that lived through the Great Depression, considered themselves lucky to get out of hard times alive. What followed World War II was an economic expansion that gave rise to the largest middle class in the history of the world and to the baby boom generation. With the economic expansion came enormous growth in the number of college graduates. If lucky children of the Greatest Generation—the boomers—got a college education and had straight teeth, their parents felt they had done their job. Our generation craved independence from our parents, and with that came the impulse to be self-sufficient. Unless there was a disaster, we didn't ask for anything more. Our parents were entitled to what they had earned—and we didn't want to be responsible for them when they got old.

The economic situation has changed radically since the turn of the twenty-first century. Many of our children and grandchildren have experienced the Great Recession. They don't have access to the same level of jobs and security that we enjoyed. Today it takes at least two full-time salaries to support a family. Day care is extremely costly, and so is everything else. Many of our adult children need our help. But we have to figure out how to do it, and that's not easy.

It's important to sit back and think about your finances. Figure out what you have, and what you owe. What is coming in and what is going out? It's sometimes hard to look money in the face, but knowledge is power. There are plenty of computer programs to help people calculate their financial situation, and for people with savings, there are financial advisers. Most advisers will tell you that your own financial security comes first. They advise grandparents to hold off sending money to the grandchildren if such gifts will put them in financial peril. They may be correct, but we also need to contend with the fact that different people have different attitudes toward money. It's an emotional hot spot for most of us. So first consider your money style.

Are you a spender or a saver? If you are a saver, over the years you may have amassed some assets. But spending? Not so easy. Money means just as many things to our generation as it does to our grown children. It means security, the yield of hard work, and safety. To part with our savings isn't easy. For spenders, the joy of being generous may be met with a harsh reality of inadequate means. Most people are somewhere in the middle. If they are part of a couple, their spending styles may differ, and that's another source of conflict. Financial insecurity and generosity don't go together, and spending down a life's savings can make one partner feel good and the other partner toss and turn all night.

Many older women tell me that they have just enough money to last until they reach this age or that. After that, who knows? If you are skating on the edge of financial trouble and you have a grandchild in need, what do you do? Do you tell your children you can't help? Do you explain why? Or do you bite the bullet, write the check, and hope for the best? For financially insecure grandparents, what may be a genuine sacrifice can be seen by grown children as commonplace generosity. When a request for help can't be met, it can be interpreted as lack of love instead of lack of means. Different sets of children and grandchildren have different needs. How to choose between helping the single mom with three children and the working daughter who has no kids? How do we cut that pie? Do we give to the needy and praise the successful? Or do we give what we have equally?

We try to solve equations with too many unknown variables. But consider these three philosophies of spending and giving.

The first says, "Sink or swim. I did it, and so can you."

This has the merit of simplicity. It makes for self-reliance. It builds character. It may not be so easy to live by if the needs of the grandchildren are seriously not being met and you have the means to help. This approach is also kind of old-fashioned, and it probably won't be appreciated in today's environment. More than 65 percent of grandparents help their grandchildren financially and many put money into the college savings accounts of their grandchildren, so you may be unpopular. It does build character—and sometimes resentment.

A second philosophy says, "I'll give more to the neediest and make up the difference later."

Think of this as Grandparent Socialism, or different strokes for different folks. If one family is struggling, and these parents cannot pay the medical bills for their child, or for the lessons or tutoring, or summer camp, or child care, grandparents who have the means often help out. Problems arise when siblings compete. Remember the app? It counts what their parents are giving each of them and calculates the difference. It lights up when one sibling gets something the other hasn't received.

Cynthia's daughters and her husband are schoolteachers in a big-city public school system. They live in an expensive city and experience financial stress. Cynthia applauds her children's commitment to public education and helps the grandchildren in every way she can. Her doctor-son's wife, a successful money manager, has the app. If she doesn't get what her sister-in-law receives, she's outraged because she thinks she and her husband should be treated equally, even if they don't need the money. Fortunately, for peace in the family, my friend has the means to even things out. Her third child, divorced, is so consumed by the struggles between his first wife and his second wife that he doesn't care much.

Sometimes the gifts of time and money merge. Joanne has a daughter who lives a thousand miles away. This daughter has three children, and a little financial help from Joanne and her husband goes a long way. She sends them a set amount each year, enough for music lessons, or sports equipment, or trips. When her son, who lives nearby, found out, he complained. "You don't give us any money for my daughter's lessons." Joanne had a ready answer: "Want me to charge you for babysitting?"

The third philosophy of giving says, "Everybody gets the same, no matter what."

I call it Granny Egalitarianism. It has the merit of being simple. But if your means are limited, like most grandparents, and your grandchildren have wildly different needs, it may be a hardship.

So perhaps it makes sense to embrace the model of a mixed economy. There's a safety net for children and grandchildren in great need, and a smaller gift for those who are secure. Competition need not be the byword here. Better to think of the family system—siblings included—as a community. Ask your grown children, the brothers and sisters who are parents to your grandchildren, to understand this framing. Explain that you expect them to have generous thoughts about each other, and that you will do your best to make sure that they are treated fairly over the long haul. So if there's a grandchild with a disability, or if one of them has serious financial troubles and is trying to work his way out of them but is in dire need, the competition app may be disabled.

The best compromise I have heard from the grandparents I have met, is this: be a socialist now, and a capitalist later—in your will. Some family members will suffer from the injustice of your disproportionate giving. Since inevitably situations change, the most accurate answer to the big question is: it depends. But if we have a pretty good idea of how we view money, and if we have told the kids about it, then changes may be less threatening. In any case, you are in charge of your financial philosophy and have every right to assert it.

No Strings Is the Rule

THE PROBLEM WITH money is that it's like a chameleon. It changes color and meaning according to the surrounding environment. The emotional weight that comes with giving across generations can harm relationships in ways we never expected. Money loaned is trouble. Money watched is control. Money given is love.

Sandra worries about her future. A social activist, she never earned much, and her savings are sparse. She counts her pennies. She's been reticent to talk about her situation with the grown children, so requests for a new bike or swimming lessons for the grandchildren trip easily off their tongues. She's sapping her reserves. But the big mistake Sandra regrets was cosigning a loan with her daughter-in-law. When the loan came due and her daughter-in-law was behind in her payments, the bank came after Sandra, who couldn't repay the loan. Her continued requests that her daughter-in-law make good on the loan almost ruined their relationship. Sandra learned the hard way the first rule of intergenerational generosity: if you make a loan to a member of your family, think of it as a gift. Don't expect to get it back.

Sometimes, in our desire to help the grown children who are struggling to become better managers of their expenses and debt, we are tempted to offer them advice that accompanies the bills we pay or the checks we write. After all, most grandparents who are lucky enough to be able to be generous have amassed that money by being careful.

We are grateful that we can be generous, but sometimes the ways in which the next generation spends our money makes our hair stand on end.

Boomer children and grandchildren are better at consuming, buying, and spending than most of us ever were. Grandparents who never took much from their parents shake their heads over today's consumerism and remember the old days when ski trips and oboe lessons were not considered necessities. The differences we notice between our lives and their needs might tempt us to comment. That's why there is a danger in paying off credit card charges. If you see what's being spent and on what, it can be hard to stay silent. Complaints about how they spend our money are useless. They turn generosity into control and breed resentment instead of gratitude.

If you are helping out, give the money as a gift and let it go. Or, if you are paying for lessons or tuition, pay the institution directly and cut out the middleman. Don't expect loans to be repaid. That takes the heat off the debt. It's a good rule for all loans, I'm told. But when it comes to loans to the children, it's a mercy to view the money as spent.

And don't expect expressions of gratitude. That way, when they come, you will be glad. If our generation has the means to help the children and grandchildren, that is an amazing gift. We can thank our hard work, our good fortune, or our lucky stars. In any event the very fact that we are able to be generous is a great reward in itself. It's a privilege to be generous.

The Conversation

A WISE AND aged stockbroker gave me this advice years ago. He was ninety-four years old and had advised many families over several generations. Sid said that once the grown children know the facts they can begin to deal with them realistically.

He told me to bring my sons together, without their spouses. Tell them what you have, what you will need, and how you plan to distribute in your will what's left. It's important to have all the adult children together, so they get the same information from you at the same time. Then invite the spouses to hear the information, too. If some adult children have a gripe with your allocation, they can say so, if not in the moment, then later. The greatest advantage of this openness is that, if they think you are being unfair, they'll blame you, not the sibling they think is getting the better deal—after you're dead.

People on the receiving end deserve to know the context from which our generosity springs. Otherwise they cannot evaluate the extent of our generosity—or sacrifice—and they won't have the information they need to be thoughtful recipients. If we want our grown children to act like adults, we need to treat them like adults. This means telling them what they need to know about our finances, our priorities, our health, and our concerns. The better informed they are, the more likely they are to be realistic about what they can expect from us, and they may even be helpful.

I sought this advice when I was writing my first book, *Walking on Eggshells,* more than a decade ago. I've shared it with many friends. Some are shocked and shake their heads. One man thought it was a miserable idea. "If they know what I have, they'll want it now." OK, I thought. But it's your money, and your decision.

Another friend tells me that she's a private person and could not imagine sharing this information. OK, I think. But you see how your children are counting and watching and worrying that they are getting less than their siblings. If she's unhappy with the rivalry between her grown children, the conversation might help. But for her, privacy is the top value. So be it.

I did convince one friend to follow Sid's advice. She and her husband sat their two grown children down and told them what they had, and what they planned to give each family every year, so long as they could. The strife is over. This conversation helped to return money to its true form, legal tender and not emotional baggage.

The Last Word

WHETHER YOU'RE A spender or a saver, a socialist or a capitalist, something will be left to be inherited—maybe just some furniture, snapshots, jewelry, and paintings.

Whatever your philosophy of giving may be, new rules apply to the will. If we want our children and grandchildren to stay close and maintain the family into future generations, the philosophy of egalitarianism is a good idea. The assets should be divided as fairly as possible. This will not necessarily make up for the different ways in which we have helped out during our lives, but if it will be seen as fair, you have done your job. Some grown children seem indifferent to our possessions, but others are emotionally attached to them. Offer them all the opportunity to identify the pieces that they would like to have after we are gone. That's the easy part.

If our descendants sit at the lawyer's table and are shocked to learn that we have left more to one child or grandchild than to another, they will be enraged. But they'll be angry with the wrong person. They won't blame us for being unfair. They'll blame the lucky inheritor. We all have seen families torn apart because of such wills, many beyond repair.

If you tell all your children what you are planning to do, you give them a chance to let you know what they think and give you the opportunity to make a change or stand your ground. One successful man I know, when he learned that his father was leaving a big asset to his more financially needy sister, felt that he had been denied his patrimony. He gathered the family together with his father and told him what he thought. The will was changed. The siblings are still speaking. The sister survived.

So take your medicine now. It might keep your family from falling apart later.

If they are angry with you, they'll tell you so, and if you don't make a change, then at least they know whom to blame.

How does this relate to the grandchildren? They are just

one generation in the great river of your clan. They need their uncles and aunts and their cousins just as much as they needed you. Your greatest legacy isn't material goods. It's the fabric of love and understanding, compassion and forgiveness that you all have woven together. It seems a pity to squander it.

PART IV

Growing Up, Growing Old

9

The Short Goodbye

Diary of a Sad Grandma

Dear Diary:

He had been showing signs of growing up for a while. I've tried to ignore them, and I think he has too. We are very close. We've seen each other every week since he was born. He's twelve now. We read together, sometimes talk, sometimes play games, or write. The time with him passes like butter. It's loving and peaceful.

He wrote me a letter from camp this July. He signed off, "I love you more than you can imagine."

He's the best male company I know. Nobody has been that easy to be around since my husband died in 2010.

Dear Diary:

Something has changed. I visited them at their house in the country, and he and his sister teased me. Then he

sang his toilet rap song: I pee sitting down, and so forth.
Over and over again. Then he and his sister ran outside
and disappeared. I was scared and upset. Losing your
grandchildren while you are writing a book on the subject
is raw. I found them at the neighbors. They said they had
told me. They were not repentant.

Dear Diary:

He's back at school, so I thought maybe I would find
my real grandson when I picked him up. We have been
studying religion at his house with a tutor for two years,
and the sessions have been amazing. Not this time. He
writhed. He looked down. He whined. The dog was at the
vet. When would he get home?

After the tutor left, I thought we would spend some time
catching up with each other—the way we have for years. And
then I would take him out to dinner—the way we have for
years.

No talk. That toilet rap song again. Jumping up and
down on the couch. And he wasn't hungry, so no dinner. I
left. The next day I brought his sister home from school.
With his laptop on his lap, this stranger nodded his head
to signal that he saw me, and barely looked up to say hello.
I'm losing him. He's turning into a teenager. I knew his
parents would suffer when this happened but I never
thought I would lose my special place, but I have. I'm
miserable.

September 14: Good news. No hug at school, but he did
come up behind me and grab me by my shoulders. We had

a fine lesson, and although he wouldn't eat dinner with me, he let me take him to the grocery to buy his meal. Maybe I will get him back.

September 21: Not so fast. He's silent and distant. Fortunately, I had to leave before dinner because I was cooking for company. This reminded me of the benefits of having my own life.

September 28: His father phoned to ask me to be less assertive during his lesson with the tutor. I shut up. It worked. The lesson went well, although the puppy was barking and chasing through the house like a mad dog. After the tutor left, I told him that the puppy is wild and needs training. Silence. Then, "It's my dog, Grandma, and this is my house." I crept away.

September 29: I took the kids to school this morning, since their parents had to leave at dawn. I was so calm and quiet you wouldn't know I existed. He put on his suit and tie, for a big day at school. I saw a young man, a handsome fellow. Not my baby anymore. I took a picture. As I sent it to his parents, I ran across some early snapshots of a snowsuited baby in a stroller. That baby is all grown up, and I have to do some growing up myself.

Yours in sadness,
A Heartbroken Grandmother

...

Gradually the face begins to morph. Angles replace round cheeks. Corners replace childhood curves. Moods swing. The running hug has been replaced by a nod and then a quick return to the computer screen. Small changes don't amount to much. And then The Moment of Recognition arrives: the young person—that adored child who returned the love in full—is a tween, about to become an adolescent.

"Just you wait." It's a curse. Remember when you thought it, but didn't say it, to your teenager—"Someday you will know how this feels. Someday your child will torture you the way you are torturing me now. Just you wait." I don't recall exactly how my husband and I survived the adolescence of our sons. I remember times at the dinner table when one of the boys was so critical of his father that I was glad I didn't have daughters to look me up and down with contempt and say, in that terrible tone, "Mother, please!" I gradually lowered my expectations and realized that my job as the mother of adolescents was to keep them in school and out of jail as long as they were under my roof. It worked. We all survived, they grew up, made lives, married, and had children.

I assumed that when the "Just you wait" moment arrived with my grandchildren, their parents would suffer, but not me. I was seriously misinformed. When the former delightful child morphs into the difficult, moody teenager, neither generation is immune. That behavior comes from their hormones, the challenges of new responsibilities, the salience of the opposite sex, and from the pressures to leave the nest and become an adult. So what's a grandparent to do? How do we survive the Second Leaving? What should our attitude to the teenager and her family be?

The first suggestion, one I think it nearly impossible to put into action, is to decide not to take the shrugs, the silences, and the looks of total embarrassment personally. It's heartbreaking when your formerly adorable and adoring grandchild asks you to walk a few steps behind her. I am mortified when told to lower my voice. How about the time my friend's granddaughter suggested that she change her shirt before going to her performance at school. What about, "Grandma, I'll go now, and you can wait in the car for a few minutes. I'll see you after the concert." If you can keep your head during these encounters, congratulations. A sense of humor and a sense of perspective are the first two tools of sanity. The third is a sense of history. Grandparents must remember that their (once) terrible teenager eventually came back as a human being. If we have true courage, we might even cast our minds back to the times when we were teenagers, driving our parents crazy, with the moods, the looks, the secrets, and the bad behavior.

I had an epiphany on a train in Norway, from Oslo to Bergen. My older son was thirteen or fourteen. The trip across the Norwegian Alps was breathtaking. I brought a book to read for the six-hour ride, but I never opened it. The scenery was too gorgeous. Every once in a while, the train would pass through an above-ground tunnel. They resembled New England covered bridges. These structures must have been placed where the snowdrifts would be the most trouble for the trains in the long winter. In this glorious summer, passing through them was to experience both dark and light. Spaces between the wooden slats allowed a little bit of sun, and then we would be in the dark again. Out of the tunnel, the magnificent scenery reappeared. Eventually we reached Bergen.

This train ride is my metaphor for adolescence. We all board the train in fine weather, and then sometimes we enter a tunnel—the child disappears—emotionally and spiritually. Then as little bits of light sift through, you get a glimpse of the young person you helped to raise. Dark and light, here and not here, this is the ride we take with our teenagers. Eventually we arrive at the last stop, and what do we find? We meet that same child, the original wonderful being—no longer a stranger, and almost grown up. The trip is over and that interesting beloved person is back again. We both have survived the trip. Much of this journey wasn't any fun. Adolescence isn't a whole lot of fun for the young person, either. Remember how miserable it was for us?

My metaphor has helped many parents of teenagers understand that the end point to a fulminating adolescence would eventually arrive. So, grandparents, remember that they will come back: wiser, better, and grown. We just have to live that long. And we will. We must.

...

As the elder generation suffers through this second set of adolescents, here are some strategies to maintain the thread of closeness with your teenage grandchildren and to be of help to their harried parents. All the strategies, all the attitudes, and all the responses can be summed up in two words: Be Switzerland.

Maintain Neutrality, No Matter What

JUST AS SWITZERLAND refused to take sides during World War II, grandparents are well advised not to take sides when the two generations are at war. A grandparent can offer a safe, neutral spot for a furious adolescent who needs to complain, cry, and stamp his feet. "That's awful," we can say to the grandchild. Then we can commiserate with the parents, "How can you bear it?" By not taking sides, we provide a place to flee the enemy and regain strength between battles. If we have established with the parents that we are trying our best not to judge them in their time of trouble, and if the grandchild knows that our love is still unconditional—even when he or she goes off the rails—then maybe we can be of help. Maybe.

Louise has two adult daughters. One lives in her apartment building and another nearby. Louise is a kind and loving lady with four grandchildren, two from each daughter. Last year, one of Louise's daughters was struggling with her

son. It just had gone too far: he never lifted his seventeen-
year-old nose from his iPhone or iPad, or iSomething. She
was beside herself, and so she put her foot down and put
the devices in her safe: he couldn't use his phone or any
other electronic device for a week. This was harsh. He
was irate. He ran away from home. Yes, he ran away to his
grandmother, Louise Switzerland. Louise was glad to offer
him a safe harbor, but she wasn't so sure about how hard
it would be to handle her furious grandson. And then she
relaxed. Poking out of his travel bag was his stuffed animal. Louise thought of it as the Runaway Bunny. That's the
thing with adolescents, one minute they're almost adults,
the next minute they need their snuggly.

Louise's other daughter is a single mom, raising her two
kids alone. She lives with her children in the same building as Louise. Recently a boyfriend entered the picture,
and her daughter asked Louise to babysit while she and
the boyfriend enjoyed a weekend in the mountains. Louise agreed. Her preteen granddaughter was happy to bunk
with Grandma upstairs. They love to hunker down in front
of the TV and munch goodies. But the teenage grandson
was not in the mood. He wanted to stay in his own room,
downstairs in his mother's apartment. The building where
they live is safe and not very large. And this grandson is a
reliable kid. So Louise became a free-range grandmother.
The boy slept alone in the apartment and didn't get into
trouble. Everybody was proud of his independence.

　　Neutrality does not rule out setting the kinds of limits

that adolescents need, even as they fight against them. So Patsy, who persevered with her teenage granddaughters, assures me that she has no trouble saying, "You can't talk to me that way, it's disrespectful. I didn't deserve that." This was her way of keeping the lip to a minimum. The limits set in Switzerland are just as irksome as those set elsewhere. And they may evoke similar distress and distain from the adolescent. But many grandparents still enjoy a special status with the kids, and the teenagers may listen to us more than they listen to their parents.

Adolescence is a hard time. The brain is growing almost as fast as it did when the child was a baby. The body is growing fast, too. The hormones are raging. And the world outside the home is becoming the (only) real world. Add to this the evolutionary urge to separate themselves from their parents and other authorities and the need to measure up to the peer group, and you get a testy, snarky, tense grandchild, who is in pain and probably feels alone, lonely, and often unlovable.

But unlike the parents, we don't have to live with them (and if we do live with them, we can go to our room and shut the door). If we are annoyed and hurt by their show of attitude and their behavior, we can disappear and thus create enough space to recover.

We also know from experience that this stage will pass. After all, we survived the years when our kids were those annoying, infuriating teenagers—and our parents survived the years when we were just as awful. We grew up, and they grew up. The attitude of neutrality allows grandparents to listen to the teenager without the emotional baggage their parents carry. And if we listen carefully, we may be able to glimpse what the teenager is going through.

Harry, a man whose wife had recently died, took a fledgling grandson to live with him at the farm when the young man was at war with his mother. Harry tells me that he set house rules for his grandson. This wasn't the best time in the world for either grandfather or grandson, but in neutral territory the teenager was able to calm down a little and count the days until he went away to college. When Harry set limits on his grandson's behavior at his house and gave him chores to do, the teenager realized that the penalty for misbehavior was to be sent back home. So he was pretty good. His grandfather also heard him out. He didn't agree totally with the boy's complaints, but he saw his point. He injected a bit of realism as he detailed some of the ways in which the teenager had helped to raise the temperature at home. Grandpa was relieved to see him go, because having a furious seventeen-year-old in the house was taxing. But he undertook these weeks as part of his grandparental responsibility. Harry was glad to help. Also helpful was the fact that the youngster was on his way to college, so everybody could count the days until the armistice. Communications from college were full of good times and excitement. Mission accomplished—for now.

...

The common, everyday arguments and conflicts between parent and teenager do not always put grandparents on guard. It's another matter when things get serious—or dangerous. When that happens, grandparents have a sacred responsibility to protect.

Dorothy has three grandsons. Because they are African-American, she worries about their safety out on city streets. Dorothy had made her son—the grandsons' father—dress neatly and behave politely when he was young. This was to protect him from gangs and other dangerous teenagers in late 1980s Los Angeles. Today she tells the grandsons to do the same.

Dorothy says, "I'm a wreck!" Her oldest grandson is a college student who has a baseball scholarship. She worries that he is in danger of DWB (Driving While Black). She cautions him to walk around his car and check out every detail before he gets in—every time. She doesn't want him to get picked up for some small infraction that might escalate into big trouble. Safety first, she cautions, even if it seems crazy. As the independent person that she is, not the voice of her grandson's parents, she hopes the teenager might just listen—and hear.

Laura was extremely close to her maternal grandfather when she was a kid. He took her fishing and taught her patience. He listened to her, and the lessons of his life are in her heart, even though he is long gone. Laura's mother was not an experienced driver, and she was anxious when Laura got her learner's permit. Laura needed to practice her driving. She and her mother would set out, Laura behind the wheel. Her mother would sit next to her, bursting with anxiety. And when it was time for Laura to slow down, her mother's foot would hit the floor, even though no brake was there. The tension in the car was unbearable for mother and daughter. Then Grandpa stepped in. He offered to accompany Laura on her practice drives. Grandpa the patient fisherman slipped into the "death seat," waited for Laura to start the car, and calmly watched and guided her as she became a proficient driver.

Laura's father plays the same role with her teenage son. When he gets rambunctious, a call from Grandpa lowers the volume in the house. I expect that when Laura and her husband become grandparents they will become temporary citizens of Switzerland, too.

This brings me to a man of wisdom with a wonderful sense of humor. He had moved in with his daughter and her family after the death of his wife. Even though he lived in the house, Poppa kept a certain distance. The door to his room was closed. If one of the grandchildren wanted to enter, they needed to knock on the door and answer the question, "Who is there?" Entry was always offered.

Stanley was the eldest grandchild and the closest to Poppa. So when he was in high school and his girlfriend became pregnant, the first knock was on Poppa's door. In this strict Catholic family of the 1960s, getting a girlfriend pregnant spelled disaster. Abortion was not an option, and he didn't love the girl. But she wanted to get married.

Stanley wept as he told Poppa his story. He was mortified, and he didn't know what to do. Poppa comforted Stanley and left the room to tell the parents what had transpired. It was a tragic mess, but they survived, mainly because Poppa offered a safe harbor for both generations. He listened to his daughter's rants through that spring and summer, and his shoulder kept her from fainting at the wedding. In truth, Poppa was excited about the impending birth of his first great-grandchild. He had a soft spot for that baby, and he watched out for her after her parents divorced.

Nobody's Perfect

LOSING IT IS part of being human, and it's hard to stay neutral all the time. Grandparents who are lucky enough to stay close to the inner workings of a complex family face special challenges when they deal with divorce, remarriage, composed families, and new in-laws who didn't come with the original package. Our natural impulse in these situations may be to step away in order to stay cool and preserve family stability. But if we are intensely engaged with the part of our family that is in conflict, sometimes we speak out and pay the price. Martha's sense of fairness overtook her wish for serenity in the family.

Martha's beloved Jack is her son's only child. When Jack was about eight, his parents divorced. Jack has been close to his grandparents since he was a baby. He spent many summers with them at the beach. It's not unusual for a child of divorce who lives with his mom to blame the father for everything. Jack is no exception. Martha held her tongue for years but reached a breaking point when Jack went after his father.

At dinner with his grandparents, Jack was complaining that his dad "walked out on a happy family." Martha snapped. She said to him, "Enough! You're sixteen. I'm telling you the truth now. It's about time you knew. It wasn't your father who walked out. It was your mother who walked out. It was your mother who was having an affair." Jack was shocked. "That's not true!" He stood up and ran out of the restaurant.

It was true, but Martha took a lot of heat. Her son was furious, and Jack did a disappearing act. How could she have done this? She admits that she lost it, but she couldn't stay silent and watch her grandson speak lies about her son. Eventually things calmed down. After all, Martha had stood up for her son (who in time appreciated her loyalty), and Jack got some facts he didn't know. Martha decided in the heat of this dinner to give up her place of neutrality. We all do this at one time or another. And our hope is that the bonds between the generations are resilient enough to allow everybody to lose it without permanent damage.

Sometimes a teenager acts like an adult, to the surprise of all. David's father died some years ago, and his mother has a complicated relationship with her former in-laws. She struggles to keep her son connected with these people, who are David's only living grandparents, even though she thinks they are self-involved and deeply annoying.

David was about to turn sixteen. Just returned from a stint as a junior counselor at summer camp, he told his mother he didn't want a party, or even the family at dinner. Just them and their best friends would be fine. No cake, no candles, no singing. So be it.

Later that week, David received an angry e-mail from his grandmother. She was hurt. Why hadn't David called her when he got back from camp? How come he didn't invite his grandparents to his birthday dinner? Why didn't he call them on his birthday? How could he be so thoughtless? She guessed David didn't really love them. This grandmother had left Switzerland for the time and had become an antagonist. David's mom fumed. A day went by.

Then David decided how to deal with his only living grandparents. He texted them, kindly and calmly. He wrote that he loved them. He suggested that they might have called him on the occasion of his sixteenth birthday. Grandma called to admit David was right, and she apologized. David asked if they could get together for lunch the following week—without asking his mother's permission. They did that, and now David sees them without his mother. David's mother will never like her in-laws, but her opinion is moot for the time being, because David has taken over the relationship.

Surprises. That's the theme of surviving the years when the once adoring grandchildren turn the focus onto themselves, their peers, and their emotions. For grandparents to leave the spotlight and become a bit player in the lives of their grandchildren is tough. Here's the consolation. They come back. At the end of what seems to be an interminable journey, a taller and more composed individual turns up—in the house, at the dinner table, perhaps on the way to college.

Precious? As precious as that baby in the stroller.

Adorable? As adorable as the one who sang the alphabet song over and over again.

Charming? As charming as the one whose eyes lit up when you came to school on Grandparents' Day.

Yours? Yes, yours again, cognizant of all the years of love, when that love was gratefully accepted, and even when it was dismissed.

Yes, nothing compares to the feeling we get from that cuddly two-year-old who wants to climb in our lap for a big hug. Since that's no longer possible, if we live long enough we still can look forward to the next chapter, the sweetest time of all.

10

The Gloaming

I told her,
"You can do that. You can do anything you set your
    mind to."
And she said,
"You know what? Your opinion doesn't count,
    because you think everything I do is perfect."
I was thrilled. I thought, "I'll take it."
—*Ali, grandmother of a twenty-something*

I treasure the moment in the day when the sun has set but there's still a glow in the sky. Some call it the Gloaming. Others call it the Magic Hour. Even though darkness is on its way, energy and illumination fill the air.

This happens in the morning, too. Just before you can see the sun rising on the horizon, the sky begins to glow. It's a harbinger of the new day. These two gloamings remind me of the precious time when adult grandchildren and their grandparents come together. One looks forward to the new day, the other faces a setting sun.

Sunrise

GRANDPARENTS NEED TO live a long time to find themselves in this position. But it's happening more and more. Today, many more college graduates have living grandparents than ever before. We live longer and healthier lives. In addition to the benefits of improved medical science, diet, exercise, relationships, and fun are all life extenders. If we are lucky enough to be close to our grandchildren, we can look forward to our time together in the Gloaming. Even if we have not been so close when they were children, we get a second chance when they grow up. We have a secret strength that helps us get close. In this day and age, we offer grandchildren something they can't get elsewhere.

Young people in their twenties and thirties are experiencing a new developmental stage, called by psychologists "extended adolescence." It usually takes another decade after college for them to settle down. Parents expect their children to find work and love in the decade after college graduation, and they are disappointed when they don't. The young adults share this disappointment. They recognize that they are far behind their parents in reaching the milestones of adulthood. They don't have career paths— and maybe they never will. In this world, a job is precious enough. A career? Maybe some time in the future, if a miracle happens.

They are slow to form permanent relationships. People

are getting married later and later—if ever. This generation is aware of how far they lag behind their parents. "At my age," a twenty-something tells me, "my mother already had us three children." Another person compares herself with her dad: "He was already at the company where he worked all his life." Lifetime marriages and lifetime jobs don't happen so much in the twenty-first century. And they know it.

So they float on a cloud of concern. Their parents are more than concerned. They are worried. Yet talking to parents about these issues can be tricky. Parents tend to get anxious. They fret. Parents give advice. They want to solve the problem. It's no surprise that many young people steer clear of serious conversations. They don't want to make their parents anxious or angry, and they sure don't want to be told what to do.

At the dawn of adulthood (which finally comes somewhere in the thirties), they need someone to talk to. They need somebody to listen, without anxiety and without criticism. This is when grandchildren can turn to those of us who may be facing the end of the day. Without trying, without getting up from our chairs, we offer them what they need.

Affection without judgment.

Plenty of time to spend listening.

A deep knowledge of the family's history.

Perspective that comes from our length of days.

No suspicion that we aren't getting the whole story.

Faith that things will work out.

Our example of survival, through life's twists and turns, aches and joys.

Recognition that we have been lost and uncertain—just like them.

Sunset

MY FATHER WAS a wise man. Surrounded by piles of books in his small study, he would spend hours discussing people, history, ideas, and politics with me. The best advice he ever gave was this. "Friends your age will grow old and die, and you'll be alone, so be sure to get to know younger people. Make younger friends. They will also keep you relevant." I followed his advice.

Today, as I walked my dog on a cool clear morning, I realize that if I live long enough, I may see my grandchildren grow into adults. Someday they might become my young friends. This hope keeps me going.

If we are old enough to have grown grandchildren, chances are that we are close to or in our fourth quarter. We face challenges that we never have experienced before. Our bodies don't act as young as we feel. It takes effort to get up and out, to fill our lives with people and experiences. Sometimes we suddenly find ourselves exhausted, looking for the nearest chair to drop into. We often wake up early and achy, hoping that by sunrise we can move all our joints. We deal with the waning of our relevance. We have lost friends and relatives, and we miss them. The only people who listen to us (if they can hear) are our old friends (if they are still here). We strain for relationships.

And then the phone rings or the cell phone beeps. It's a grown grandchild, checking in. We're needed again, if only for a meal or a kind word, or help of some sort. They have the energy, the experiences, the crises, the problems, and the need for our attention. We don't especially irritate them by our quirks—they shrug them off the way our grown children never could. They want someone to listen just as we crave their company.

There's no single version of these relationships. Sometimes we offer grown grandchildren, through our passions or our interests, a model of behavior that isn't like anything else in their lives. We seem comfortable in our way of being in the world, and they find us comforting. Robyn, who struggled with depression, always found a smile from her grandmother, a woman who knew that Robyn would be OK.

Grandma Taps Her Way through Life

ROBYN WAS CLOSE to her father's parents all her life. Grandpa is an amazing man, and she spends more time with him now that Grandma is gone. But Grandma was her idol, her model, and her source of amazement. This grandmother didn't win any Nobel Prizes. She wasn't a world traveler or a crusader for human rights. She was a character. When Robyn grew up, she would meet her grandmother for lunch near the office. The restaurant couldn't be too close to where she worked, because Robyn didn't want her colleagues to witness Grandma's antics. She signaled the waitress by waving her hand in the air. Her voice would carry across the room. She would arrive at the table with a hatbox or shopping bags brimming with clothing—more like costumes—for Robyn. She loved hats and colorful clothing, and she insisted on giving her favorites to her favorite granddaughter. Robyn had to try the hats on at the restaurant.

Grandma embodied joie de vivre. When she was fifty, she took up tap dancing, and it became the passion of her life. She took classes all the time. She practiced all over the house. She tapped in amateur theatrical and dance productions in her area. One winter Robyn and her father were at a ski resort with Grandma. The cabin was a duplex, and the bedrooms were downstairs. Early one morning, before breakfast, Robyn and her dad heard a strange noise. Was it a woodpecker? No, it was Grandma, now eighty, tapping her way through the upstairs kitchen.

Grandma's high spirits were a source of energy for Robyn, who struggled with the blues. Grandma, by her very being, would cheer her up. Here's a famous family story. When her hearing began to fail, Grandma got hearing aids, but they didn't work very well. One day Grandma and Robyn's father were in a store.

"She was talking to my dad, and the checkout woman

was ready for her, saying, 'Can I help you? Can I help you?'
And my dad turned and said, 'She doesn't hear you, you
know? She's deaf. She doesn't hear you.' But she heard him
in her good ear, and she smacked my dad."

Robyn tells me this story with laughter in her voice.
This woman was a sketch, a model of take-no-prisoners
confidence and joy. Grandma never lost confidence in
Robyn's future. She outlined clear goals for her granddaughter: be joyful, take chances, and enjoy every moment
you can. Her grandmother's upbeat view of the world was
a blessing for Robyn.

Even when Grandma was diagnosed with lung cancer,
she didn't flag. Robyn's father said it. "Well, she's still
dancing, and as long as she can dance, she's fine. Just
keep her dancing." Only when her body was riddled with
disease, and her breathing was limited, did she stop.
And then she quit eating and drinking. Robyn went to
see her. "She was vain. And when I went to go see her,
she looked beautiful. She had her makeup done, and she
was in her beautiful peasant shirt. She loved clothes and
dressing up, and I don't think she wanted people to see
her sick, or not looking her best." Robyn put her face close
to Grandma, so she could hear. "She wanted to know if I
was happy, and I was able to tell her all good things about
my relationship." Then "it was wonderful. I was able to
hold her hand and just try and project my love from my
face to hers. And I told her, 'I love you so much. You're just
the best grandmother ever, and I adore you.' And she said
it back to me, and everything that needed to be said was
said."

This may serve as encouragement to those of us grand-parents who don't fit the mold. Our grown children may cringe and frown in embarrassment, but somebody out there loves us—for all the good and all the strange. Feel better now? I do.

Quirky grandparents come in all shapes and sizes, all cultures and all cuisines. Helen reaffirmed her closeness with Yia Yia when she was a college student. Their affinity was confirmed in London and continues across the Atlantic Ocean to this day.

Safe Harbor

HELEN'S GREEK GRANDMOTHER picked her up from pre-school when her mother was at work. She lived with the family for a few years before returning to London, where Helen's grandfather ran their business. The family spent summers in Greece together. I can see the sun on Helen's face as she describes those summers. Helen and her sister grew up, her grandfather and uncle died, and Yia Yia settled into a quieter life in London. The cloud of age descended. She couldn't travel as much as she neared her eighties. But Helen and her sister could. They both took time to study in England.

Helen was lucky. She was able to spend an academic year at Oxford, and she planned to spend her weekends with Yia Yia. Helen doesn't think she could have survived the year without Yia Yia. It turned out that her academic work was infinitely more demanding than anything she had experienced in college. She was studying philosophy and politics, and she had a tutor. That's very different from sitting in a lecture hall and taking notes. The first week, Helen had a reading list of twenty books. She sagged into Yia Yia's apartment that weekend. It was a shock to both of them. Helen couldn't spend the time with her grandmother that they both had expected. She had to study. She had to read and then write her papers. Helen admits that she wasn't much fun, as she ping-ponged her weekends from her desk to the dining table, and then back to work. Yia Yia was disappointed, but she adjusted. Now their conversations weren't about boys and parties. They were about what to eat. Yia Yia was so happy to have her beautiful granddaughter with her every weekend that she settled for food. There was a lot of it. Plenty. More than plenty. Portion size became a source of conflict, but not the cause of a rift.

Yia Yia, a round Greek grandmother clad in black, thought that when you finished your plate of food, it was time for a refill. Helen was watching her weight. None of this mattered. They loved each other, and in return for the safe harbor she offered Helen, her grandmother sopped up the energy and life that her granddaughter brought into her small London flat. The two thrived. Helen says she couldn't have lasted the year without Yia Yia, and she tells me that her grandmother's mood was much lighter by the time she left for home.

Now, back in America, Helen keeps up the connection.

There's a five-hour time difference between grandmother and granddaughter, so when Helen walks to work in the early morning, it's lunchtime in London. Helen places a call. What do they talk about? Nothing much—except food. What do they share? They share what psychologists call affinity, "emotional closeness and consensus of opinion." Research is beginning to show that this relationship across the generations is good for everybody's mental and physical health. Are you surprised? I'm not. The funny thing about affinity is that it doesn't necessarily have to begin at the cradle. Sometimes the two generations meet again across a cup of coffee, or perhaps sitting together in the theater.

The Pleasure of Your Company

MARGARET DIDN'T SPEND much time with her grandchildren when they were children. She had her kids young, and they had their children young, so Margaret was still working and supporting the rest of her family when the next generation arrived. No time for babysitting, not too many long walks or board games. But she loved all seven of them and visited with them when she could.

A successful businesswoman of many interests and passions, she spent part of the month working in New York City and the rest of her time in a small town out west. As the grandkids grew up, she invited them to visit her in the big city. Some didn't want to come. They were not that close to Margaret, and furthermore, the Big Apple could be intimidating. But her grandson Daniel wanted to be an actor. So a visit to Grandma was a trip to Mecca. He would stay for a week and they would go to the theater every night. Margaret's new husband was delighted to get to know this stepgrandson who turned out to be curious about everything and full of fun. For years they looked forward to Daniel's visits, and then the best thing happened. He was accepted into an acting program in New York. Now they feed him, too. They all explore neighborhoods in search of fine dining at a bargain. Margaret loves to walk the city with her grandson, as they form the golden bond.

Margaret's story tells us that affinity can appear under all kinds of circumstances. Grandparents don't need to have spent every day or week or month with a grandchild to discover that easy, comfortable, and joyous relationship with a grown grandchild. It can come as a great surprise.

Affinity is one of those things that's hard to define and impossible to predict. But when it happens, you know it.

Janet tells me that her twenty-four-year-old son rushes to spend a Sunday afternoon with his grandfather. She asks him how they fill the time. What do they do? First they catch up on each other's lives. They listen to each other's stories, complaints, successes, and adventures. The young man and the old man feel free to put anything on the table without fear of being judged. Maybe they read the paper or have a nosh. Maybe a nap. Companionable silences are sometimes interrupted by a comment. Love and a sense of ease fill the room without words. This sounds like heaven to me. It is the completion of a relationship that began when a grandfather held a tiny, feather-like newborn in his arms. Now, decades later, the mutuality of affection and regard sustains them both.

Aristotle, in his great work *The Nichomachean Ethics,* considered friendship the highest form of human interaction. Being the close observer he was, Aristotle described three forms of friendship, the lowest being a relationship based on utility. The middle form—one that I have just described, happens when people are drawn to each other's good qualities. The finest form of friendship, according to my favorite philosopher, is friendship based on goodness, where both people admire the other's goodness and help one another strive for the highest level of good.

Imagine what Aristotle would have had to say about Gabriella and Sylvia, Betty and Carl.

Sylvia's Coffee

GABRIELLA COMES FROM an immigrant family that keeps its generations close. Her father's mother was her favorite. She and her sister would spend summers visiting them in their New York City housing projects apartment where they lived. The sisters played with the other children on the grounds beneath Grandma's window. When they needed something, the kids would yell up to the open window, and down would come a bag of cookies, or a candy bar. Those summers in the city bring a warm smile to Gabriella's face.

But she didn't care for her other grandmother. Whenever Gabriella and her mom visited Sylvia, things got tense. Her mother would weep all the way home. This grandma had a sharp tongue that often wounded Gabriella's mother. Gabriella didn't choose to see much of Sylvia by herself. They had no bond that mattered.

Things changed when Gabriella moved to New York after graduate school. As it happened, Gabriella worked and lived near Sylvia. A blend of curiosity and a sense of unfinished business led Gabriella to get to know her. And what did she find? A friend. A woman fifty-five years older than she, a person who knew her family very well, and the repository of family stories and secrets that Gabriella was dying to learn.

They had a ritual. First came the coffee, "the best coffee in the world," Gabriella tells me. Then they would have a snack: crappy crackers and low-salt cheese, with a bit of leftover ham or turkey from one of those supermarket packets.

Then would come the paperwork. Sylvia was by then getting a bit vague (and a lot sweeter), so her granddaughter would go through the accumulated mail and also handle her medical paperwork. By now a medical school administrator and teacher, Gabriella became an expert in the ins and outs of the health care system by helping her grandmother.

Then they would talk. Gabriella needed to know about her mother's family, and why her mother and Sylvia didn't get along. These were dark conversations, but they were important. The secrets came out. Sylvia's husband was a brute, who began to beat his wife a week after the wedding and who also beat his children. The sad family stories explained so much to Gabriella. Truth became the grounding element in their relationship.

Truth telling goes both ways. Gabriella didn't know whether Sylvia comprehended her granddaughter's sexuality. Once they drove to the suburbs to visit dear old girlfriends of Sylvia's.

On their way home, Gabriella said, "Grandma, do you realize what you just did?" "No, what? Tell me?" "You just took me to your friends' house and they're a couple. Was that your way of telling me you're OK with me?" Sylvia didn't own up to it then, but Gabriella got the message.

Later, as she was nearing the end, Sylvia asked her granddaughter, "Kiddo, when are you going to find a man?" She said, "Listen, Grandma, you know what? You find men attractive. I find women attractive." Sylvia nodded her "OK."

And then there were adventures. Sylvia, who by now lived in an age-assisted apartment, loved to shop. She would take her granddaughter to the supermarket to ferret out the bargains, and to CVS. There, she would actually bargain over prices with the salespeople—and win. They would have lunch at McDonald's: fish sandwiches and french fries. Sylvia knew every street in the Bronx. "She could have been a cabdriver," Gabriella tells me. And she was intrepid: fun, funny, sharp, and unstoppable.

And that coffee. All Sylvia needed to do was call and say the pot was on, and Gabriella would be there in a flash.

A heart attack took Sylvia just days after she turned eighty-five. Gabriella tells me, "When we cleaned out her apartment, I took the things that she made the coffee with—as my own memory—and I took my coffee mug." Gabriella was an adult when she discovered Sylvia, who was already an old lady. Family, plus affinity, plus age, may equal the highest form of friendship.

The Prodigal Grandson

BETTY IS EIGHTY and her oldest grandchild, Carl, is twenty-five. First grandchildren have a special place in the hearts of many grandparents, and Carl is no exception. She babysat when he was small, stayed with him after school, went to his baseball games, took him to the movies, and hosted the teenage parties when he was in high school (she locked herself in the bedroom during the parties). They were so close. Partly because his parents were divorced and his mother worked long hours, Betty took extra pains on Carl's behalf.

Then he grew up. First, he dropped out of college. A smart kid, he told his family that school was boring and useless. Unfortunately, Carl had no Plan B. He moved to the apartment in his mother's garage and slept late into the afternoon. Who knows what he was smoking. The family fretted. Then he found a girlfriend who had a shady past. They met her once. Once was enough.

Carl noticed the disapproval heading his way. He took the natural steps for a twentysomething in his situation.

He all but dropped out of the family. He stopped replying to invitations and communications from his family. No conversations, no visits, nothing. An occasional text or two, to let them know he was still alive, but that was it.

Over time the separation abated, and Carl would call or write or sometimes drop by for a visit. But he refused to rejoin the family. He would not attend Sunday dinners, picnics, or birthday parties. None of Betty's other grandchildren went through these convulsions. Betty felt as if her grandson had divorced her. They had been so close. It was terrible.

Carl was still emotionally entangled with the girlfriend and couldn't break free. His attempts to start a business floundered. But he wasn't about to go to his family for help: he was abashed and ashamed.

So Carl did a smart thing. He moved across the country to a large city on the East Coast. Now his absence from Sunday dinners and other family occasions was no longer the cause of conflict. Distance helped him disengage from the girlfriend. He started a new life and a new business.

As he began to get his life together thousands of miles away from his family, Carl gradually returned to his grandmother. Betty would be a good person for him to talk things over with. She's no business magnate, but she knows a thing or two. And she has the time to talk and talk. She doesn't evaluate his financial success the way his father does, and she doesn't fret about his social life like his mother. Betty just listens, encourages, laughs, and sends love long-distance. He calls her two or three times a week.

I found a place for the office.

I have a great apartment.

I think things are going OK.

Made a couple of friends.

We're going hiking this weekend.

This guy wants to make a deal. What do you think about
it?

For Betty, these conversations are like the icing on a
cake. She's relevant again. Her opinion counts. She's up-
to-date in his life. She can share in his modest successes,
after all those years of worry. That old affinity, hidden for
so many distressing years, has reappeared. And it has
morphed into friendship.

The joy of sharing life with the next generation also
means that they have much to teach us, and we have much
to learn. The famous gift of the youngest generation is
their knowledge of technology. Just ask a grandchild, and
our computer or iPhone problems are solved. They might
even have the patience to sit with us while our brains
slowly adjust to this new knowledge. The grown grandkids and their friends are immersed in a culture we don't
know intimately. They can teach us. They may be working in fields we don't know much about. They may have
traveled to exotic places that we never visited. They have
stories. Their intimate relationships may be entirely

different from ours. We can learn about all the ways to love.

At the end of our long conversations in his book-lined study, my wise father would say, "Janie, I loved our talk. There's nothing so sweet as learning from your child." How much sweeter is it to learn from your grandchild. Our lives are enriched as we enrich their lives. We create for each other a safety net of love and concern.

At a recent get-together with close friends, we talked endlessly about grandkids and about what it feels like to grow old. That night I had a dream.

A Grandmother's Dream

I WAS IN the middle of the ocean. Lost at sea, I swam as hard as I could, coasting over some waves, and fighting others. In the distance I could make out a bit of land with palm trees. "A desert island," I thought.

The swells carried me toward the shore, and when they relaxed, I swam harder. But I was getting tired and I couldn't tell if I could ever reach land. Swell, stroke, breathe, swim, stroke, breathe, was I getting there?

Yes. I let the smaller waves wash me ashore.

Where were the palm trees? Nowhere to be seen. In their place stood my grown grandkids, beckoning me to a safe harbor.

EPILOGUE:
"GRANDMA, I'LL ALWAYS VISIT YOU"

On a hot July afternoon, I was discussing my upcoming birthday with Ruby, age six. We were sitting side by side in a booth at the diner where we have dinner after I pick her up from day camp.

"I'll be seventy-five," I said. We nodded to each other. That's old. I had been warned not to discuss the party plans with her (I didn't know why, but I try to follow the rules), so we were shaking our heads about what a big number seventy-five is. Ruby took a bite of her pancake. There was a pause.

"I'll always visit you," she said, her face grave with promise. I cocked my head in question.

"Visit me?"

"When you're in the place. I'll visit you even when you're in a wheelchair."

I got it. Ruby was thinking beyond that big birthday, to the time when I would be old, and infirm. "You'll visit me even when I can't pick up my head?" I asked, bobbing with an open mouth. "Even then?"

There was a pause. Ruby, serious the way a six-year-old can be, said, "Grandma, I will always come to see you. I will."

It was the best birthday present I'll ever receive.

ACKNOWLEDGMENTS

Imagine the joy of writing a book on this subject while being surrounded by your grandchildren. My first thanks must go to this amazing quartet, Benjamin, Ruby, Tobey, and Mazie, for showing me how to be a grandmother—and how to grow as they grow. Next, I must thank their parents, my sons, Dave and Josh, and their amazing wives, Jennifer Gonnerman and Cathie Levine. They have folded me into their homes and lives. And every day I learn from them.

There are many ways to learn. One is by doing—that's the grandchildren. Another is by talking—and listening. So for the endless, regular conversations about our grandchildren, our children, and everything else, including this book—I thank Naomi and Tina. Where would I be without you?

Mary Pipher and I have spent twenty-five years trying to figure out together what life and family are all about. We share each other's work, and Mary's comments on the draft of this book changed it immensely—and for the better. Thank you, Mary, for this and for so much else.

Celina Ottaway, my friend and teacher, urged me (actually she forced me) several summers ago to write from the heart, as well as from the head. That was hard for me, but it opened up levels of strength for which I thank her.

Latifa Fletcher, brilliant graduate student, surveyed the psychology and sociology literature about grandparents and three-generation families. I'm grateful to Tia for opening the door to what social science has to say about family.

Heidi Wald, friend and neighbor, sat with me in the early days of this book, encouraging me with stories from her life and from the lives of her friends. She brought me the first focus group and has been a bright light in my life. Sara Gilliam brought me another focus group. Thanks, Sara. Jackie Patnode, thank you for opening your home to me and for gathering a group of grandmothers to share their stories and wisdom. Susan Newmark, wise friend, brought me to the Jacob Riis Settlement house to meet an extraordinary group of grandmothers and great grandmothers.

Thanks to all the men and women I interviewed—grandparents, parents, and grandchildren. I hope I have done credit to what you have taught me. (I have changed your names and altered some details to protect your privacy.)

I want to thank Jake Hass, Bailey Georges, Michael Sesling and his crew at Audio Transcriptions for their faithful and timely help.

Gail Winston is a brilliant editor. When this book works, it's thanks to her.

Hugh Van Dusen started this off, at a miracle lunch at the Union Square Café. How can I thank you enough, old friend?

And Liz Darhansoff? She's always there, when you think you need her, and when she knows you need her. Magic.

Alexandra Fahrni listened while I thought aloud, asked wise questions, and through our conversations made me think harder and better. I wish she were here to read this book.

NOTES

....

Introduction: Stardust

3   On grandparents living longer: Lindsay M. Monte, "Fertility Research Brief: Current Population Reports," SIPP Research Brief P70BR-147, U.S. Census Bureau, Washington, DC, 2017, https://www.census.gov/content/dam/Census/library/publications/2017/demo/p70br-147.pdf.

5   grandparents move near their children and grandkids: Quoctrung Bui and Claire Cain Miller, "The Typical American Lives Only 18 Miles from Mom," *New York Times*, December 23, 2015, https://www.nytimes.com/interactive/2015/12/24/upshot/24up-family.html.

9   *The Hidden Life of Trees:* Sally McGrane, "German Forest Ranger Finds That Trees Have Social Networks, Too," *New York Times*, January 29, 2016, https://nyti.ms/2k8cdB5.

Chapter 1. Grandparent Prep: What to Do Before the Baby Comes

28   "the good-enough mother": Daniel Winnicott, *The Child, the Family, and the Outside World* (New York: Basic Books, 1964; Penguin, 1973), Chapter 2.

Chapter 2. When Everything Changes: The Shift of Power

31   Can you tell when you become an adult?: Julie Beck, "When Are You Really an Adult?" *Atlantic*, January 5, 2016, http://www.theatlantic.com/health/archive/2016/01/when-are-you-really-an-adult/422487/.

35   On mother-daughter and mother-son differences: Melissa A. Barnett, W. Roger Mills-Koonce, Hanna Gustafsson, and Martha Cox, "Mother-Grandmother Conflict, Negative Parenting, and Young Children's Social Development in Multigenerational Families," *Family Relations: Interdisciplinary Journal of Applied Family Studies* 61 (December 2012): 864–77, doi: 10.1111/j.1741–3729.2012.00731.x.

Chapter 4. The More They Know, the Taller They Grow: The Impact of Family Stories

75   On children benefitting from learning family history: Marshall P. Duke and Robyn Fivush, "The Stories That Bind Us: What Are the Twenty Questions?" *Huffington Post*, March 23, 2013, updated May 23, 2013, http://www.huffingtonpost.com/marshall-p-duke/the-stories -that-bind-us-_b_2918975.html.

83   On talking with Rose Kennedy and memory: Doris Kearns Goodwin: she told us this story at a Simon & Schuster sales conference in Boston, in 1985, the year before the publication of her book *The Fitzgeralds and the Kennedys: An American Saga*.

Chapter 5. Our Fountain of Youth

90   On the positive effects of grandfather-grandchild involvement: James S. Bates and Alan C. Taylor, "Grandfather Involvement and Aging Men's Mental Health," *American Journal of Men's Health* 6, no. 3 (2012): 229–39, doi: 10.1177/1557988311430249.

94   lowered risk of Alzheimer's: Solveig Glestad Christiansen, "The Association between Grandparenthood and Mortality," *Social Science & Medicine* 118 (2014): 89–96, doi: 10.1016/j.socscimed.2014.07.061.

101   more concerned about losing their memory than losing their looks: Catherine Marienau, "My Role Models Worry More about Losing Their Minds Than Their Looks," *Women's eNews*, April 19, 2016, http:// womensenews.org/2016/04/my-role-models-worry-more-about -losing-their-minds-than-their-looks/.

104   Grandparents are living longer: Lindsay M. Monte, "Fertility Research Brief: Current Population Reports," SIPP Research Brief P70BR-147, U.S. Census Bureau, Washington, DC, 2017, https://www .census.gov/content/dam/Census/library/publications/2017/demo /p70br-147.pdf.

Chapter 6. Love and Sacrifice: Custodial Grandparents

124   On the stresses of grandparents raising grandchildren: Tara García Mathewson, "More Grandparents Are Raising Grandchildren. Here's How to Help Them," *Hechinger Report*, September 2, 2016, http:// hechingerreport.org/parent-substance-abuse-incarceration-drives -increase-in-grandparents-raising-grandchildren/.

Chapter 7. Staying Close While Living Far Away

126 On grandparents choosing to live near grandchildren: Harriet
Eldleson, "Grandparents Who Move to Be Closer to Grandchildren,"
New York Times, June 26, 2015, https://nyti.ms/2k4Bb04.

Chapter 8. Who Gets What and When?

160 More than 65 percent of grandparents help their grandchildren
financially: Ana Veciana-Suarez, "How Grandparents Give . . . and
Give . . . and Give to Their Grandchildren," *Miami Herald*, January 17,
2017, http://www.miamiherald.com/news/business/personal-finance
/article126962309.html.

Chapter 10. The Gloaming

188 "extended adolescence.": J. J. Arnett, *Emerging Adulthood: The Winding
Road from the Late Teens through the Twenties* (New York: Oxford
University Press, 2004).

198 On friendship: Aristotle, *The Nichomachean Ethics*, translated by
David Ross (Oxford: Oxford University Press, 2009).

FURTHER READING

Chapter 2. When Everything Changes: The Shift of Power

Dubas, Judith Semon. "How Gender Moderates the Grandparent-Grandchild Relationship: A Comparison of Kin-Keeper and Kin-Selector Theories." *Journal of Family Issues* 22, no.4 (May 2001): 478–92.

Eisenberg, Ann R. "Grandchildren's Perspectives on Relationships with Grandparents: The Influence of Gender across Generations." *Sex Roles* 19, nos. 3–4 (1988): 205–17.

Chapter 3. Nurturing the Moral Imagination

Copen, Casey, and Merril Silverstein. "The Transmission of Religious Beliefs Across Generations: Do Grandparents Matter?" *Journal of Comparative Family Studies* 38, no. 4 (2007): 497–510.

Pratt, Michael W., Joan E. Norris, Shannon Hebblethwaite, and Mary Louise Arnold. "Intergenerational Transmission of Values: Family Generativity and Adolescents' Narratives of Parent and Grandparent Value Teaching." *Journal of Personality* 76, no. 2 (April 2008): 171–98. doi: 10.1111/j.1467–6494.2007.00483.x.

Chapter 5. Our Fountain of Youth

Ben Shlomo, Shirley. "What Makes New Grandparents Satisfied with Their Lives?" *Stress and Health: Journal of The International Society for the Investigation of Stress* 30 (2013): 23–33. doi: 10.1002/smi.2492.

Chapter 6. Love and Sacrifice: Custodial Grandparents

Hughes, Mary Elizabeth, Linda J. Waite, Tracey A. LaPierre, and Ye Luo. "All in the Family: The Impact of Caring for Grandchildren on Grandparents' Health." *Journal of Gerontology: Social Sciences* 62B, no. 2 (2007): S108–S119.

Livingston, Gretchen, and Kim Parker. "Since the Start of the Great Recession, More Children Raised by Grandparents." *Pew Social Trends*. September 9, 2010. http://pewrsr.ch/X1od3i.

Pruchno, Rachel. "Raising Grandchildren: The Experiences of Black and White Grandmothers." *The Gerontologist* 39, no. 2 (1999): 209–21.

Rankin, Sonia Gipson. "Why They Won't Take the Money: Black Grandparents and the Success of Informal Kinship Care." *Elder Law Journal* 10 (2002): 153.

Strom, Paris S., Robert D. Strom. "Grandparent Education: Raising Grandchildren." *Educational Gerontology* 37, no. 10 (2011): 910–23. doi:10.1080/03601277.2011.595345.

Chapter 7. Staying Close While Living Far Away

Forghani, Azadeh, and Carmen Neustaedter. "The Routines and Needs of Grandparents and Parents for Grandparent-Grandchild Conversations over Distance." In *Proceedings of the SIGCHI Conference on Human Factors in Computing Systems*, 4177–86. New York: Association for Computing Machinery, 2014. doi: 10.1145/2556288.2557255.

Mäkelä, Ann, Verena Giller, Manfred Tscheligi, and Reinhard Sefelin. "Joking, Storytelling, Artsharing, Expressing Affection: A Field Trial of How Children and Their Social Network Communicate with Digital Images in Leisure Time." In *Proceedings of the SIGCHI Conference on Human Factors in Computing Systems*, 548–55. New York: Association for Computing Machinery, 2014. doi: 10.1145/332040.332499.

Mueller, Margaret M., Brenda Whilhelm, and Glen H. Elder Jr. "Variations in Grandparenting." *Research on Aging* 24, no. 3 (May 2002): 360–88.

Chapter 9. The Short Goodbye: Taming Teenage Grandkids

Creasey, Gary L. "The Association between Divorce and Late Adolescent Grandchildren's Relations with Grandparents." *Journal of Youth and Adolescence* 22, no. 5 (October 1993): 513–29.

Dunifon, Rachel, and Ashish Bajracharya. "The Role of
Grandparents in the Lives of Youth." *Journal of Family Issues* 33,
no. 9 (2012): 1168–94. doi: 10.1177/0192513X12444271.

Chapter 10. The Gloaming

Fischer, Claude S. "Grandparents Today." *Boston Review*. October 19,
2015. http://bostonreview.net/blog/claude-s-fischer-grandparents
-today.
Gentile, Olivia. "Does How Often You See Your Grandkids Affect
How Long You Live?" *Grandparent Effect*. January 5, 2017. http://
grandparenteffect.com/does-how-often-you-see-your-grandkids
-affect-how-long-you-live/.
Ruiz, Sara A., and Merril Silverstein. "Relationships with
Grandparents and the Emotional Well-Being of Late Adolescent
and Young Adult Grandchildren." *Journal of Social Issues* 63, no. 4
(2007): 793–808.
Silverstein, Merril, and Anne Marenco. "How Americans Enact
the Grandparent Role across the Family Life Course." *Journal of
Family Issues* 22, no. 4 (May 2001): 493–522.

A Note on Sources

So much of my point of view is in my bones. I grew up in a house of Freudians, edited and published books on psychology and child development for nearly half a century, and by inclination and profession kept up with much of the literature. Latifa Fletcher helped me by searching out the contemporary research that's relevant to this book, as you will see from the citations above. But the thinkers who have been most important for me in the writing of this work are Erik Erikson's *Childhood and Society*, John Bowlby's great trilogy on attachment, and Donald Winnicott's work on mothers and children.

INDEX

....

ABOUT THE AUTHOR

JANE ISAY is the author of *Secrets and Lies*, *Walking on Eggshells*, and *Mom Still Likes You Best*. As a book editor for more than forty years, she discovered Mary Pipher's *Reviving Ophelia*, commissioned Patricia T. O'Conner's bestselling *Woe Is I* and Rachel Simmons's *Odd Girl Out*, and edited such non-fiction classics as *Praying for Sheetrock* and *Friday Night Lights*. She lives in New York City.